For my dearest friend _Fr. Al_,

with lots of love,

Babs

Christmas, 1997.

Imre Madách

THE TRAGEDY OF MAN

Translated from the Hungarian by
GEORGE SZIRTES

Introduction by George F. Cushing
Illustrations by Mihály Zichy

CORVINA

Original title: *Az ember tragédiája* (1860)

Translator's Note by George Szirtes
On Mihály Zichy by János Falus, translated by Christina Rozsnyai

Designed by János Lengyel

Published by Corvina Books Ltd.
Budapest, V. Vörösmarty tér 1. Hungary 1051

Second edition, 1995

ISBN 963 13 3994 7
Printed in Hungary, 1995
Szekszárdi Printing House, Szekszárd

INTRODUCTION

Imre Madách and The Tragedy of Man

The Tragedy of Man is the most controversial work in the long history of Hungarian literature. When it was first published in January 1862, it was hailed as a great achievement, but at the same time it gave rise to a multitude of questions, both literary and philosophical, that have been fiercely debated ever since. It is also one of the most surprising works in Hungarian: it appeared suddenly from the pen of an unknown author and had no obvious antecedents in the Hungarian literary tradition. Moreover there is nothing, apart from a passing reference to Hunyadi in Scene 14, to brand it as Hungarian—a unique phenomenon at a time when Madách's contemporaries were agonizing over the failure of the revolution of 1848 and its repercussions on national life and expectations. How then did a Hungarian country gentleman who spent most of his short life at home and rarely travelled outside his native county come to write a dramatic poem that takes its place in a broad European tradition represented by such giant figures as Milton, Goethe, Byron and Ibsen?

There is no straightforward answer, for Madách left no diary and no early drafts of his work. Only one manuscript of *The Tragedy of Man* has survived, together with a scrap of paper indicating a running total of lines in each scene, the names and number of characters and the dates between which he wrote it. His earlier unpublished works and correspondence provide a few clues to his thought, but his family and narrow circle of friends had no idea of what he was writing in the 'Lion's Den', as he called his study, between 17 February 1859 and 26 March 1860. His home was in the small village of Alsósztregova, now Dolná Strehová, Slovakia, which lies in the foothills of the Carpathians only sixty miles due north of Budapest as the crow flies, but light-years away from the capital in all other respects. The county of Nógrád in which it lies was renowned in the nineteenth century for its sleepy conservatism, decaying estates and the impoverished and eccentric gentry so admirably described in the stories of Kálmán Mikszáth (1847–1910), himself a native of the area. Alsósztregova had been the seat of the Madách family for centuries when Imre Madách was born there in 1823, the third child and eldest son in a family of five. His home, a modest neo-classical mansion set in an extensive park, was then new, built by his grandfather to replace the 'old castle' which still dominated the village. The older Lutheran and newer Catholic churches both contain Madách memorials, for the same grandfather had reconverted to Catholicism. Madách's father died in 1834, leaving his determined widow to manage the scattered estate of some 9,500 acres and bring up her large family, which she did with strict economy, for the estate was heavily in debt, but also with due regard to the social conventions of the age. The children were thus educated at home by a succession of tutors, their mother's French companion and visiting teachers of art, music and dancing. The house contained a large and wide-ranging library of books mainly in German, but also including works in Latin, French and Hungarian, both classical and contemporary. This remained a civilized haven for Imre Madách, whose health was always poor; he devoted much of his time to reading.

In 1837 Imre and his two younger brothers were sent to Pest to continue their education there; they were accompanied by a tutor and a housekeeper who maintained the strict economy they had known at home. Imre was to pursue the legal studies then customary among the country gentry. But he found himself in the exhilarating atmosphere of a city full of ideas concerning reform, and it was the youth who were discussing and promoting them. In a country where literature played the part of the opposition in a democratic parliament, there were new and outspoken ventures in writing and what was to become the National Theatre had just opened. Madách soon became friends with fellow-students who later became political leaders; he joined in eager debates, fell in love for the first time and turned his hand to romantic lyric and drama. Three of his poems appeared in 1839 in the literary journal *Honművész* and in 1840 he published at his own expense a volume of 26 poems entitled *Lantvirágok* (Lyre Blossoms) for his relatives and friends. The theme of this book is his hopeless love for Etelke Lónyay, the sister of one of his friends, yet it is dutifully dedicated to his mother, who strongly disapproved of the attachment, since Etelke was a Protestant. The poems display little else but a talent for imitation, but a letter of the same year reveals a depth of feeling and maturity of thought unusual in a teenage youth.[1]

Madách returned home in 1840 to enter the legal service of his county while continuing his studies. There he was popular, though his career was interrupted by visits to spas to seek relief from the heart and respiratory troubles that plagued him. He turned again to writing, this time in the form of drama. He wrote several plays on Hungarian historical themes, cumbersome in structure and awkward in language, none of which were published or reached the stage. There was also a new cycle of love-poems to Lujza Dankó, who died of tuberculosis in 1843, but once again these display more the results of his familiarity

6

with the romantic idiom of his age than original talent. Much more intriguing is an essay on art which reveals his deep knowledge of Greek drama, an unusual accomplishment in a country where classical studies are generally restricted to Latin, and one shared with his contemporary and later mentor János Arany.

In his daily life Madách, who returned from Pest full of reforming zeal, encountered the frustrations of the backward-looking and cumbersome administration of his home county and was delighted to find a like-minded friend and lifelong confidant, Pál Szontágh. Their correspondence sheds light on Madách's otherwise reserved character. There was a latent satirical streak in him which was encouraged by Szontágh's ironic wit. One by-product of their association was a collection of epigrams on the county administrators, including themselves. Madách is characterized thus:

> You're a liberal now, with good connections and learning;
> That's why you hold your little snub nose so high.
> Just wait a bit till you're the deputy lieutenant of Nógrád:
> Your principles will melt away—and you'll still hold your nose up high.[2]

It was probably Szontágh who introduced Madách to journalism, inspiring him to write a series of critical articles on county affairs for the influential newspaper *Pesti Hírlap*. Here he cloaked his radicalism under the pseudonym "Timon", borrowed from the French publicist Cormenin-Timon, whose work he admired. But in the county assembly he spoke openly on free trade, the reform of the electoral system and the abolition of the death penalty, themes current in Pest but hardly appreciated in Nógrád. In 1843 ill-health forced him to resign his post as deputy notary, whereupon he was accorded the title of county court judge. He continued to write, though none of his poems, short stories or dramas was published then. Only one play, *Csak tréfa* (Just a Joke), is of interest as revealing his perpetual struggle as a radical against the pettiness and servility he found around him. Otherwise, at most his activity shows his interest in dramatizing history and evaluating the role of women in society.

In 1844 he met his future wife Erzsébet Fráter at a county ball. He was in the depths of depression, and she seemed to him to lift him out of himself. He fell madly in love with her and courted her despite warnings from his friend Pál Szontágh and the objections of his mother, who pointed out that she was flirtatious, of lesser rank and, what was more, a Protestant too. At that time she was seventeen, a lively and passionate girl who was also highly neurotic. The marriage took place in 1845, and the young couple made their home some twenty miles away in the village of Csesztve; their estate was still Madách property, but ironically part of the disapproving mother's dowry. At first all was happiness. Although their first son died in infancy, three more children, a boy and two girls, were born to them. But tensions began to develop; Erzsébet did not share her husband's frugal tastes and love of learning. She proved moody and extravagant. Matters became worse when the revolution of 1848 broke out and Madách became involved in it. In 1846 he had been elected to the post of chief commissar for the county, in peacetime a sinecure. But in time of war it involved arranging supplies for troops stationed in the county, a considerable task in an area of poor communications. Apart from a brief spell in the spring of 1848 Madách, who was wholeheartedly on the side of the revolution, held this post throughout the conflict, despite his poor health. His two brothers also offered their services to the revolutionary government, and kept him well informed of events. Here at last the discussions and debates of earlier years had given place to action, and hopes ran high. But tragedy soon struck, both nationally and personally. Not only did the revolution fail, but the Madách family was shattered by the death of Imre's brother Pál, a dispatch-carrier (whose features Madách incorporated in his painting of St. Sebastian in the Catholic church at Alsósztregova), and then by the murder of his sister Mária and her second husband at the hands of bandits. They left a young son whom Imre was to bring up with his own family. Then the father of his surviving brother's fiancée was hanged, the penalty for serving in the Ministry of Finance of the revolutionary government, and his friend Pál Szontágh was sentenced to two years in prison.

The cumulative effect of these disasters was deep and lasting. In the poems he wrote at this time there are several pointers towards *The Tragedy of Man*. "Life is a struggle, death repose," he writes in one verse, which ends: "I may fall in the struggle, but never shall I make a deal with fate."[3] And in a poem commemorating the death of his sister he has harsh words for the ingratitude of the masses when individual heroes sacrifice their all for them, a theme which recurs in the Athens scene in *The Tragedy of Man*.[4] Madách himself was next to suffer for his part in the revolution and its aftermath. In 1851 he gave shelter to János Rákóczy, a distant relative who had been secretary to Kossuth and was under sentence of death. Rákóczy carelessly gave himself away but managed to escape from his pursuers, while Madách was arrested and imprisoned first in Pozsony (now Bratislava) and then in Pest. The revenues from his estates were also confiscated. Meanwhile his wife had to fend for herself and her family; her mother-in-law was unhelpful, as her increasingly desperate letters to her husband indicate. He returned home in August 1853 to discover that she had been unfaithful to him during his imprisonment and that his marriage was virtually in ruins. A further problem was that his mother had decided to hand over the estate to her children; this meant that Imre Madách and his family moved back to Alsósztregova, where his mother still lived in the 'old castle', offering endless possibilities for further family friction. His marriage finally broke down in 1854 when a divorce was agreed. Madách retained custody of his son and younger daughter, while his estranged wife went to her home with the elder daughter. This settlement did not last, since she was unable to provide properly for her daughter, and eventually the children were reunited in the Madách home.

Imre Madách now became increasingly withdrawn, devoting most of his time to reading and writing in the 'Lion's Den'. He maintained contact with a few local friends, notably Pál Szontágh and the two village clergymen; there were also further flirtations, duly recorded in verse. But his mood of despair at the fate of Hungary and at his own personal tragedy persisted. In this he was not alone. The wave of optimism that had preceded the revolution had given way to general self-questioning and doubt, against the background of harsh Austrian reprisals. How had things gone so wrong? Who was responsible? Above all, what was the future in store for the country? Other writers were seeking the answers to these problems in a sober reconsideration of the immediate past and a cautious glance at a necessarily gloomy future. This was the atmosphere in which Madách in his isolation pondered the ideas that eventually emerged in *The Tragedy of Man*. Once more there are clues in his poetry. *The Creation of Woman* depicts an Eve who "scatters blessings and curses" like her counterpart in the drama.[5] His versification of the Biblical story of Cain and Abel not only shows that he had read Byron's *Cain,* but also indicates his own state of mind, for he makes "freezing intellect" the real murderer, and this is a phrase that, with variations, recurs in *The Tragedy of Man* where Lucifer's rationalism repeatedly dashes down Adam's romantic idealism.[6] Two letters in verse to Pál Szontágh also betray his mood: the first, dated 11 August 1856, contains an attack on marriage, while the second, of 7 February 1857, is a terrible cry of despair,[7] on the draft of which he wrote, "I have re-read the poison poured out for Pál. Why haven't I kept it to myself? Why not? This poison is the truth, even if it's tragedy too, and human nature has never denied itself, and Adam from the time of creation onwards keeps appearing in different guises, yet basically he remains the same feeble worm at the side of the even feebler Eve."[8]

Such evidence as this demonstrates how Madách was gradually putting his own tragedy into a much wider setting and trying to draw general conclusions from it. His reading included epics dealing with the fate of mankind and contemporary works on the advance in natural sciences and the philosophy behind them. Works on social progress, biological determinism and entropy (foreshadowing the cooling-down of the sun and the degradation of the universe) all formed part of his studies. The only clues to his reading at this time, apart from those found in *The Tragedy of Man* itself, are scraps of paper on which he noted quotations and ideas, both his own and those of others, that intrigued him. These cover an immense range, but how deeply he read is another matter. Different philosophical concepts jostle each other throughout his work, as do different scientific ideas, while the Phalanstery scene interprets Fourier's work in a way that its author would not have recognized.

Before he completed *The Tragedy of Man* Madách wrote yet another play, totally different from any of his other works. *A civilizátor* (The Civilizer) is a short Aristophanic comedy presenting a sharply satirical view of the post-revolutionary political scene in Hungary. It displays a new-found dramatic skill based on a good knowledge of Greek comedy, and is of particular interest here as a demonstration of his ability to break away from Hungarian literary traditions. Not surprisingly its theme made it unpublishable, but it deserves recognition as an indication of the mood of the period and as a document of its age.

Of the actual writing of *The Tragedy of Man* there are no records or reminiscences. When it was complete, Madách set it aside and soon began work on a new Biblical drama, *Mózes,* in which the hero is once again confronted by the ungrateful masses. Later he read *The Tragedy of Man* to his friend Szontágh, who suggested some emendations and urged him to send it to János Arany, at that time the most influential figure in the Hungarian literary world, for an expert opinion. Meanwhile Madách came out of his retirement to play an active role in politics, as if the completion of his dramatic poem had helped him to come to terms with himself. He was elected a member of the Diet, where his few speeches revealed him as a thoughtful and effective orator. While in the capital he sent *The Tragedy of Man* to Arany, who glanced briefly at it, noted some infelicities of language and prosody in the first few pages and put it aside in the belief that it was a poor imitation of Goethe's *Faust.* But in May 1861, after the enthusiastic reception of a speech by Madách on the constitutional position of Hungary, Arany was persuaded to look once again at the manuscript. He discovered that his earlier opinion had been mistaken; his enthusiasm grew until finally he wrote to Madách offering his help with improvements in vocabulary and versification, all with the aim of rapid publication. Madách was delighted; he confessed that he would have burnt his work if Arany's opinion had been negative. So the first edition, with Arany's emendations, was published in January 1862 (though dated 1861), and it brought immediate fame to Madách. Literary honours were heaped on him, but at the same time he was subjected to severe criticism, the precursor of the controversies which still continue. Some of the first critics questioned details, which induced Madách to correct them for the second edition of 1863. This is now accepted as the standard text.

Madách continued to write. He completed his play on Moses and submitted it for a prize, but it was rejected. Some of his earlier poetry was published, and he was assembling a collection of it when death came on 5 October 1864. His reputation therefore rests solely on *The Tragedy of Man*.

*

The structure of Madách's dramatic poem—he did not call it a drama, though its conception is dramatic—is straightforward. Of the fifteen scenes, the first three are Biblical, set in heaven, paradise and outside paradise respectively. Scenes 4 to 14 contain Adam's visions: the first four of them are rooted in ancient and medieval history, from Egypt to Byzantium, then follow three linked scenes set in Prague with a forward vision of the French Revolution. The last historical scene depicts contemporary London. Scenes 12 to 14 deal with the future and end of humankind, separated by an attempt to escape from earth into space. The final scene reverts to the place outside paradise as Adam wakes from his dream.

The first three scenes follow a pattern familiar to readers of Genesis and *Paradise Lost*, but with subtle variations to suit Madách's purposes. Lucifer is established as a sarcastic critic of the creation and is allowed not one but two trees in Paradise, those of knowledge and immortality; these, he confidently believes, will enable him to work on Adam and wreck the divine order. He tempts both Adam and Eve to eat of the first tree, but they are prevented from sampling the second and driven out of paradise. The third scene sees them nostalgically attempting to construct a new life outside paradise, and Adam demands that Lucifer keep his promise to impart knowledge. He wishes to know the fate of mankind, as indeed does Eve. The result is a fearsome vision of the physical and chemical processes governing the earth (as known to mid-nineteenth-century scientists), which scares Adam, since he cannot cope with them. Lucifer then summons the Spirit of the Earth to protect Adam and Eve, but instead of the gentle youth he had known in heaven, he is a terrifyingly powerful figure in his own sphere and only partially to be known to humans. Adam then demands to know why he suffers and what the meaning of suffering can be, so Lucifer puts him and Eve to sleep in order to dream the future. Here it is worth noting that the action is triggered by thirst for knowledge, not the disobedience of *Paradise Lost*. And it is significant that Lucifer, well aware of the tribulations that lie ahead, allows Adam and Eve a tiny ray of light called Hope, offering an escape from the despair which concludes each scene.

The next four scenes establish the pattern of all Adam's visions, the pursuit of an ideal which is shattered. In Egypt he appears as a youthful despot yearning for eternal fame at whatever human cost. Faced with an individual example of that cost—and with Eve—he is brought to realize the vanity of his hopes and determines to work for a democratic ideal. But in the home of democracy, Athens, he is the hero Miltiades, now misrepresented and condemned to death by the fickle masses who have been roused against him by demagogues. Eve, as his wife, curses them, and he tells Lucifer to take him to some new place where, away from lofty ideals, he can pursue a sensual life. The scene changes to Rome, where he enjoys the profligate pleasures of a young patrician against a background of death and pestilence. He grows dissatisfied, and when the apostle Peter prophesies the destruction of such a degenerate society and preaches a new ideal of brotherhood, he seeks a new world of chivalrous virtues where woman too shall be exalted. He is transported to Constantinople at the time of the Crusades. As Tancred, the leader of a troop of Crusaders returning wearily from Asia, he finds that the ideals for which he has fought have turned sour; Christians are engaged in hair-splitting petty disputes and charges of heresy fly thick and fast. Eve, who appeared in Rome as a prostitute, is now a noble woman; despite Adam's deep love for her she is compelled to enter a convent, not of her own volition but because of her father's vow. As at the end of the Athens scene, Adam desires to get away from the masses and rest, his ideals shattered once again.

In each of these scenes he is a heroic figure who parries Lucifer's often sarcastic challenges. The confrontation between them is to be seen as an argument in Madách's own mind between romantic ideals and cold logic, and to this end he takes considerable liberties with historical fact. Miltiades, for example, was not executed, nor were the Crusades, the debate on the nature of Christ and the selling of indulgences contemporaneous. Madách's approach to history is that of the good epic poet; he would have subscribed to Arany's theory of 'epic credibility', the poet's right to adapt history for his own purposes, provided that the result is credible in the eyes of the reader.

The following three scenes mark a change. Adam is now older. He leads a life of contemplation as Kepler, the Astronomer Royal in Prague. But he is forced to divide his activities between the real science of astronomy and the false one of astrology in order to please his master, the Emperor Rudolf, and his extravagant and unfaithful wife, who cannot understand his attachment to scholarship. He longs to know more of the eternal laws of science which will eventually bring a new age to sweep away the 'worn-out lumber' of the world he inhabits. He is vouchsafed a sudden vision of the future: the French Revolution has indeed swept away the old world, and Adam as Danton once more faces the masses, who are thirsting for blood. He attempts to save the life of Eve, the sister of a young aristocrat, but she is killed, to reemerge as a woman of the masses who has killed a conspirator and demands her reward—to spend a night with the great Danton. As he begins to recognize, to his horror, the features of the young aristocrat's sister in her, another mob enters to denounce him, and he goes to the scaffold after prophesying that Robespierre, his accuser, will follow him within three months. He wakes again in Prague, to reflect on his horrible vision and to instruct a pupil in the limitations of science—a scene superficially reminiscent of the dialogue between Mephistopheles and the student in *Faust*. Abstract theory is deadening; independence of thought and freedom of speech are the real goal.

These three linked scenes are by far the most personal ones in *The Tragedy of Man*, indeed some critics have been led to believe that they were written as part of a different work. Adam, the scholar and recluse, is close to Madách's heart, and Eve is clearly modelled on his wife. Moreover the role of Lucifer is reduced almost to extinction. The vision of the tarnished ideals of the French Revolution and the role in it of the masses is prompted by the Hungarian Revolution of 1848 and its failure. Revolution in itself was not evil in Madách's eyes; his political pronouncements provide evidence of his longing for a new revolution in Hungary.[9]

Scene 11 is set in Dickensian London, where Adam and Lucifer observe from the Tower the bustle of a large market. This is the world of free competition, where everything has its price and values have become corrupted and debased. Eve appears as a girl whose mother seeks a good marriage for her, and sharply rejects Adam's advances when they first meet, for he is dressed as a workman; when, however, she is led to believe that he is a rich man in disguise, she welcomes him. The rich oppress the poor and even the beggars quarrel. Adam is disillusioned once again, and demands to be led to a place where intellect rules, but before this happens the scene is transformed into a macabre dance of death round an open grave into which all the characters leap. Eve alone is saved, the eternal woman led on by love, poetry and youth to the skies. Thus Madách, in by far the most colourful and kaleidoscopic scene, ends his historical survey of the progress and failure of mankind with the grim prospect of a whole society digging its own grave. If there are overtones of Hogarth in this scene it is not surprising, since one of his caricatures hung in the house at Alsósztregova.

13

The last three visions move away from history to the future. The first of these is inspired by the work of the Abbé Charles Fourier, who envisaged socialist communities of some two thousand people living together in a Phalanstery, directed by scientific knowledge, and working peacefully and happily together for the common good. Madách, however, adopts Fourier's framework without his vision. Adam and Lucifer, as visiting scientists, are introduced to a world where initiative and individuality have given place to total uniformity, and all who step out of line are punished. Among these Adam recognizes Plato, Luther and Michelangelo. Only what is deemed useful to society is permitted, so there is no room for art and poetry. Since human life on the earth has a limited future, a scientist is trying to create life, but his experiment is shattered by the Spirit of the Earth. Now Eve appears as a mother whose children are due to be taken from her to be trained according to the rules of the community. She protests, and Adam defends her, finally offering to marry her, but this is against the scientific principles governing the Phalanstery: love has no place in this environment. Adam and Lucifer leave this inhumane world of intellect to reappear in space, flying rapidly away from the earth, doomed as it is to cool down. But this too is disastrous, since man cannot exist there in a world of spirits and God has forbidden it. The Spirit of the Earth recalls Adam, and after a brief attempt at resistance he demands to return, for life with all its suffering is better than annihilation. Lucifer tries hard to dissuade him, recalling his failures in previous incarnations, but Adam is determined:

> I know that I will fail and fail again.
> I don't care. After all, what is the goal?
> It is the end of an honourable contest.
> The goal is death, but life consists of struggle.
> The struggle in itself must be the goal.

So Lucifer takes him to earth in its last days, when only a few degenerate Eskimos are struggling for existence. Adam is now old and crippled, yet he and Lucifer are regarded as gods and implored to send more seals and fewer humans into the world. Adam is horrified to recognize Eve in the wife of an Eskimo, and asks Lucifer to release him from his dreams.

The final scene finds Adam outside paradise once more, bewildered and broken by his visions of the future. Lucifer tempts him to defy God by committing suicide, for this will prevent them from becoming reality. As he prepares to do so, Eve tells him that she is to be a mother, thus frustrating his purpose; she also foresees the birth of another child who will bring brotherhood on earth. Now Adam submits to God in words reminiscent of those of Job, and Lucifer angrily realizes that he has lost the battle. The Lord appears in glory, and Adam plies him with questions which, however, remain unanswered. Eve is to be his guardian and companion, while Lucifer's icy intellect is to act as leaven to foment rebellion in him, though not for all time. The work ends with the Lord's injunction to Adam to strive on (thus confirming Adam's realization in the space scene that life is a struggle and the struggle itself is the goal) and to have faith.

*

Madách did not live long enough to reply to the numerous questions that critics raised when *The Tragedy of Man* was published. Nevertheless there are two letters which offer a glimpse of the way in which his mind was working. The first was addressed to János Erdélyi, who had written a lengthy criticism in consecutive numbers of the short-lived political daily *Magyarország*.[10] Erdélyi accused him of pessimism, particularly in his account of utopian socialism and in his insistence on the decline of humankind. What Madách had written was rather *The Comedy of the Devil* than *The Tragedy of Man*. Madách replied:

> Your accusation suggests that I was trying to make socialism an object of scorn. The fundamental idea of my whole work is intended to be this: when man breaks away from God and begins to act relying on his own strength, he pursues this course through a succession of the greatest and most sacred ideas of mankind. True, he fails everywhere, and what causes his failure everywhere is a weakness that lurks in the innermost recesses of human nature; he is powerless to shake it off (in my humble opinion, this would be tragedy) but, though in his despair he believes that all his efforts so far have drained his energy, his development has always continued to go ahead; humanity has conquered even if the struggling individual has not recognized this, and the guiding hand of divine providence makes up for the human weakness he cannot overcome by himself. It is to this that the "Strive on and trust" of the last scene refers. Then I have tried to arrange the separate scenes or circumstances consecutively, in such a way that they follow each other as if from psychological necessity as far as *one particular* protagonist is concerned. Maybe I have not succeeded in doing this at all, indeed I fear so. I merely want to make the point that when you accuse me of mocking socialism you may also accuse me of doing the same with liberty, Christianity, learning, free trade and all those ideas in each part that I have chosen deliberately because I regard them to be the main features in the development of mankind. This is how I regard socialist ideas too, and that is why I have included them in one scene. It is true that Adam fails in each one. But he fails because of the intangible weaknesses that exist in his nature and that only the hand of God can make up for; the idea continues to develop, it becomes victorious and is ennobled. In all this my aim has simply been to rescue my intentions in your eyes; I wanted to rehabilitate the man in me, certainly not the artist. I would rather have written a bad *Tragedy of Man* in which I have not succeeded in stressing great and sacred ideas than a good Comedy of the Devil in which I held them up to ridicule.[11]

The second letter was to Károly Szász, many of whose critical observations led Madách to make changes in the text of the second edition of *The Tragedy of Man*. Szász asked him why he had omitted the Reformation, which surely counted as an important stage in the history of mankind. Madách wrote:

> I entirely agree with you, indeed this truth occurred to me while I was writing, but I decided that in the tragedy I could not make use of the Reformation as something that conquered, for if I had used it I should also have been compelled to end with the same sort of disillusionment as in the other scenes; in other words it would not have suited my purpose.[12]

These comments demonstrate the working of Madách's mind as he wrote, and it is interesting to note that his reply to Erdélyi shows yet again his knowledge of Greek tragedy in which the hero has an inherent weakness. But many problems remain unanswered, among them Madách's negative view of the role of the masses (and here it is important to note that they are not to be identified with any particular social class), or the relationship between the three main characters. Why does Lucifer's role suddenly diminish in the Prague and Paris scenes, and why are Eve's reincarnations so inconstant? The confrontations between Adam and Lucifer, as already suggested, reflect the arguments in Madách's own mind between the idealist whose faith had been severely shaken by the tragedies he had endured and the well-read rationalist whose satirical and potent reasoning nevertheless fails to break his questing spirit. The Lord's instructions to Lucifer in the last scene suggest that the arguments are to continue, but under the watchful eye of divine providence. Eve may be seen as an embodiment of Madách's experience of woman as a disappointment and an ideal—and it is the latter who finally accompanies Adam into history; here she has much in common with Milton's Eve at the end of *Paradise Lost*. She is also based on much study, for Madách had long been interested in the role of women. When elected to the Hungarian Academy he chose as the subject of his inaugural lecture (which he was too ill to deliver) 'Woman, particularly from the aesthetic point of view'; in it the references ranging from Lao-Tzu and Homer to contemporary European authors demonstrate both his fascination for the subject and his breadth of reading. It would be wrong to limit his portrayal of Eve to his own experience of a dominating mother, a neurotic wife and several flirtations.

Madách's insistence on the progress of humanity despite repeated failure, so emphatically reiterated in his letter to Erdélyi, and his inclusion in the drama of the tiny ray of hope—how he would have appreciated that once popular picture of Hope by G. F. Watts—suggest a possible link with Hungarian tradition. The poet Mihály Vörösmarty (1800–1855), himself troubled by the contrast between idealism and reality, reflected on the problem in his sombre poem 'Thoughts in the Library' (1844). After a catalogue of failures, he writes:

> And yet, and yet we must strive.
> A new spirit begins to win its way,
> A new direction breaks through men's souls.

and later:

> What is our task in the world? To struggle
> And give nourishment to our souls' desires.

This he repeats with a variation:

> What is our task in the world? To struggle
> For the noblest aims as our strength permits.[13]

Like his contemporary Arthur Hugh Clough, Madách believed that the struggle was not in vain.

The last scene has probably caused more controversy than anything else in *The Tragedy of Man*. Why, after the long succession of failures in Adam's dream, should there not be a pessimistic conclusion? Here it must be remembered that the end of the work is the beginning of history, and that Madách had selected his material carefully so that each scene would end in disillusion; as his letter to Szász indicates, he had not included significant events in the history of mankind that did not fit his plan. And in Madách's own time there was ample evidence of the progress of man; if this was less obvious in post-revolution Hungary, it was nevertheless clear in the rest of Europe, which is where Madách's reading took him; the scraps of paper containing his thoughts and aphorisms show his preoccupation with the subject. The fact that the Lord leaves Adam's questions unanswered is a reason for him to strive further, and he has been shown to possess an ever-questing spirit even at the time of his worst failures. Moreover in the last scene he regains the favour of the Lord and is given Eve as a guide. All these are reasons for optimism. If there is an ultimate aim for mankind, it would appear to be brotherhood (the 'fraternity' of the French Revolution), and this is foreseen by Eve when she refers to the birth of Christ. There is then something to strive for under the guiding hand of divine providence, a message consistent with the Catholic teaching that Madách had long before assimilated, though without the mention of redemption.

Thus *The Tragedy of Man* is very much a product of its age, a time of doubts and developments that led to re-examination of previously held beliefs. It reflects one man's attempt to think through the confusion that surrounded him. The result is a mosaic of ideas, not a consistent philosophical scheme, gleaned from a variety of recognizable sources but fused together in his mind. Sometimes the burden of the ideas is almost beyond Madách's capacity to express them and his imagination fails to match them. When he tries to be dramatic, his weaknesses become only too evident; his powers of invention are limited and his characters tend to be stereotypes borrowed from his reading. But there are moments of beauty—Eve's brief speech at the end of the London scene is one of them—and of great drama. Madách is at his best in kaleidoscopic scenes like those set in Constantinople and London.

Although Madách describes *The Tragedy of Man* as a dramatic poem, he envisaged it as a play, with suitable stage directions. The problems of producing what is in effect a series of consecutive scenes without a development of the plot are considerable. The highly compressed arguments are difficult enough to read and, indeed, re-read, and tend to be lost at a single hearing on the stage. Moreover the sudden changes of scene and the inclusion of supernatural elements present formidable technical problems. Nevertheless *The Tragedy of Man* was first staged in Budapest in 1883 and has become part of the permanent repertory of the Hungarian theatre, allowing producers ample scope for ingenuity. It has also been performed with great success in Prague (where the French Revolution scene was received so enthusiastically that the Austrian authorities promptly banned it in 1892), Vienna and the German-speaking lands, Poland, Slovakia, Croatia, Estonia and the Soviet Union; a puppet version was performed in Paris in 1937, and it has also been broadcast in various European countries and the United States. It is on record that Beerbohm Tree had plans to stage *The Tragedy of Man* at Her Majesty's Theatre in 1899, but nothing came of them.

Madách would have been astonished at the lasting interest evinced in the work he conceived in the isolation of Alsósztregova, as well as at the flood of books and articles that offer new interpretations and comments. The fact that *The Tragedy of Man* continues to fascinate and provoke new generations is an indication of both its greatness and its relevance in an ever-changing world.[14]

G. F. CUSHING

NOTES

1 M. Győrffy, "Madách kiadatlan levelei" [Unpublished Letters of Madách], *Irodalomtör-
ténet*, Budapest, 1959, 85–87.
2 *Madách Imre összes művei* [Collected Works of Imre Madách], ed. G. Halász (hereafter
ÖM), Budapest, 1942, II, 1186.
3 "Csak béke, béke" [Just Peace, Peace], ÖM II, 328.
4 "Mária testvérem emlékezete" [In Memory of My Sister Mária], ÖM II, 342.
5 "A nő teremtése"[The Creation of Woman], ÖM II, 188–191.
6 "Az első halott" [The First Dead Man], ÖM II, 140–142.
7 ÖM II, 986–988 and 989–990.
8 K. Horváth, *Madách Imre*, Budapest, 1984, 158.
9 E. g. "Politikai hitvallás" [Political Creed] and "A választás után" [After the Election],
ÖM II, 683–684.
10 "Madách Imre: Az ember tragédiája" [Imre Madách: The Tragedy of Man], *Magyarország*, Budapest, 28 August–2 September 1862.
11 Madách to Erdélyi, 13 September 1862, ÖM II, 876–877.
12 Madách to Szász, 18 March 1863, ÖM II, 947.
13 "Gondolatok a könyvtárban" [Thoughts in the Library], *Vörösmarty Mihály összes
művei* [The Complete Works of Mihály Vörösmarty] III, ed. D. Tóth, Budapest, 1962,
103–104.
14 For a fuller discussion of *The Tragedy of Man* see Dieter P. Lotze, *Imre Madách*, Twayne
Publishers, Boston, USA, 1981.

THE TRAGEDY OF MAN

SCENE 1

In Heaven. THE LORD, *resplendent in His glory, sits upon his throne, the* ANGELIC HOST *kneeling before Him. The four* ARCHANGELS *are standing beside the throne. Intense light.*

ANGELIC HOST

Glory to God in the highest,
Heaven and earth do both Him praise,
Who with one Word brought all things into being
And continues to uphold them with His gaze.
He all Power, all Knowledge and all Rapture,
We the merest shadow of His splendour,
O come let us adore him in His Grace
Of which we may partake by His sweet tender.
The Eternal Concept is made flesh, behold
The consummation of His will to form
As from His creatures now The Lord awaits
Appropriate homage to His Seat of State.

THE LORD

It's done, the great act of creation.
The maker rests. The wheel's in motion
And will rotate upon its axle for
A hundred million years before
A single cog wears out. Take wing
My sentinels, begin your orbiting.
Once more let me admire and hear the sweet
Sound of your circuit, smooth beneath my feet.

The Guardian Spirits of the stars pass by the throne, rolling before them one or two planets, comets and nebulae of various colours and sizes. The music of the spheres is faintly heard.

Look at that brave ball of fire:
So overweening its effulgence,
Unaware it merely serves
Some distant galaxy's indulgence.
   This you'd think a feeble lantern
A winking-blinking little planet,
But O how huge it seems to those
Unnumbered souls that thrive upon it.
   Two spheres contend with one another,
Rush close, repel and sharply veering
Spin away. Their opposition
Steers them through such wild careering.
   Terrifying all observers,
Thunderously one helter-skelters
Downward—yet what peace and joy
It offers to those hordes it shelters.
   How humble is this other's bearing—
A star of love in preparation,
Tender be the hands that nurture
Humankind's own consolation.
   There worlds labouring to be born
Here the tombs of worlds departed:
A warning to the overweening,
Encouragement for the faint-hearted.
   A monstrous comet hurtles madly
Out of chaos to disaster:
But see! it mends its crooked motion
When bidden by its Heavenly Master.
   Come beloved, youthful spirit
With your changing sempiternal
Sphere of woe and celebration,
Cloaked in white or green and vernal.
High heaven shower blessings on you,
Onward, undaunted: what collisions
Your narrow shores are doomed to witness,
What wars, between conflicting visions.
Fair and foul, and tears and laughter,
The winter's and the spring's endeavour,

Constitute the light and shadow
Of our Master's wrath or favour.

The Guardian Spirits of the stars withdraw

Archangel Gabriel

Thou who compassed the infinitudes,
Creating matter out of nothing,
And with one word wrought out of matter's being
Both measure and weight, we offer to Thee
Our hosannas, Concept Eternal.

He falls to his knees

Archangel Michael

Thou who fused the changeless and the changing,
Establishing both perpetuity
And time itself, uniting entity
And nationhood, we offer to Thee
Our hosannas, Power Eternal.

He falls to his knees

Archangel Raphael

Thou flood and fountain of our happiness,
Bringer of the body to self-consciousness,
Allowing the entire world to partake
Of Thy wisdom, we offer to Thee
Our hosannas, Virtue Eternal.

He falls to his knees.
Silence

The Lord

You there, Lucifer, proudly standing apart,
No word of praise from you? Are you still silent?
Does something in my work, perhaps, displease you?

LUCIFER

And what should please me? That certain substances,
Having been imbued with properties
Of whose existence You were ignorant
Until, perhaps, they revealed themselves to You,
(Though it may well be You had no power to change them)
Are now screwed up into these tiny globes
That chase, attract or else repel each other,
Awaking a few worms to consciousness
Till all of space is filled at last, grows cold,
And only the indifferent slag is left?
If man's at all observant he'll concoct
Some hash like this with his poor instruments.
Having placed him in your cosmic kitchen
You now indulge his bungling awkwardness,
His godlike postures, his botched cookery.
But when he comes to spoil your favourite dish
You'll flare up in a rage—too late by then.
But what can You expect from such a dabbler?
What is the point of the whole exercise?
A poem of self-praise is all it is—
You match it to this feeble hurdy-gurdy
And listen to the same old weary tune
Whine on and on in endless repetition.
Is it becoming to Your ripe old age
To play with this contraption fit for children?
A spark of life within a little clay,
A simulacrum, not a faithful likeness;
Free-will and fate in mutual pursuit:
It lacks all harmony, all sense of meaning.

THE LORD

I merit praise alone, not condemnation.

LUCIFER

I only render what is in my nature.

This wretched crew will serve to flatter You,
Not surprisingly since they're Your creatures.
You begat them as light begets a shadow
But I had pre-existence, and am ageless.

THE LORD

Such impudence! Were you not born of matter?
What power had you before? What sphere? What realm?

LUCIFER

I might perhaps enquire the same of You.

THE LORD

What here is bodied forth into existence
Had life in me before the dawn of time.

LUCIFER

You never sensed that void in Your conceptions,
That barrier to every mode of being
Whose very presence compelled You to create?
That barrier was one named Lucifer,
The underlying spirit of negation.
You triumphed over me since it's my fate
Incessantly to fail in all my struggles
But then, revitalized, to rise again.
When You made matter I gained my estate;
There stands life, and there beside it, death,
Joy on the one hand, discord on the other,
Shade follows light, and doubt succeeds to hope—
And see, I'm always with You everywhere.
Knowing You as I do, why pay homage?

The Lord

Out of my sight, you spirit of sedition!
I could destroy you utterly—but no,
Fight on, abhorred, in exile, in the mire,
Forbidden every solace of the spirit,
And in your bleak and anguished solitude
Let this one thought be an eternal torment:
However you may shake your chains of dust
Your struggle with the Lord is doomed to failure.

Lucifer

No, not so fast—I won't go just like that,
You can't discard me like a broken tool.
We are both creative spirits—I demand
My portion.

The Lord
scornfully

Just as you wish. Look down to earth:
In the heart of Eden stand two slender trees.
I curse the pair of them: now they are yours.

Lucifer

No wonder you are mean, you have the means.
The merest patch of ground will do for me.
A foothold I require, no more, you'll see,
To sow negation and spread anarchy.

He sets off

Angelic Host

Out of the sight of God, accursed traitor!
All praise to the Almighty Legislator.

SCENE 2

Paradise. Centre stage the Trees of Knowledge and Eternal Life. Enter ADAM *and* EVE, *surrounded by various animals, tame and trusting. Through the open gates of Heaven shines the light of glory. Soft harmonies of the* ANGELIC HOST *are heard. Bright, blazing sunshine.*

EVE

Ah life, how sweet to be alive!

ADAM

The lord and master of the world!

EVE

To feel that they are fending for us,
That all we need to do is show Him
How bounden we are to His favour.

ADAM

To lean on others is your law, I see.
I'm thirsty, Eve. Just look how temptingly
That fruit leers down at us.

EVE

I'll pluck it with my hand.

THE VOICE OF THE LORD

Beware! beware! The whole wide world is yours
But those two trees you must shun.
An alien spirit guards their tender fruit,
And those who taste it find their life undone.

Look there instead—wine ripening in clusters
And temperate shadows offering relief
From the high parching brilliance of noon.

ADAM

A strange command. How stern it seems.

EVE

Why are those two trees more lovely?
Why are they the ones forbidden?

ADAM

Why is sky blue or grass green?
That's just their way. Let's heed the voice.
Come along, Eve, follow me.

They settle in an arbour

EVE

Lay your head against my breast,
I'll gently fan you while you rest.

A violent gust of wind. LUCIFER *appears among the leaves*

ADAM

What's that? I've heard nothing like it.
I feel as if some foreign force
Had broken bounds.

EVE

I tremble, Adam.
And heaven too has fallen silent.

ADAM

I hear it still within your breast.

EVE

When clouds obscure the eye of heaven
I see it still within your eyes,
And where else should I hope to find it,
Than in you whose deep desire
Begat my birth. You are the sun
Who at his peak pines all alone
And paints his image on the water
Flirting, flushed, with his companion
Who in his bounty fast forgets
That she is but the palest fire,
A mere reflection who must fade
To nought at night with his own shade.

ADAM

Hush now, Eve, you will abash me.
What is a voice if no one hears it?
A beam without its bead of colour?
What would I be were you absent?
My life unfolds in you, a flower,
My voice resounds in you, an echo.
How learn to love myself without you?

LUCIFER

Why should I listen to these soft endearments?
I'll turn away in case I am dishonoured;
My cold and calculating intellect
Might fall to envying such childlike spirits.

A little bird begins to sing on a nearby branch

EVE

O Adam, can you understand
This little lover's clownish lisping?

ADAM

I've heard the twittering of waters.
Their song was similar to his.

EVE

What miracle, what harmony,
So many words with but one meaning!

LUCIFER

Why delay? Now rouse yourself.
Ruin I vowed, they must be ruined.
And yet again I hesitate:
Will knowledge be the way to woo them
Or ambition to assault them,
These whom tender feelings tend
And harbour like a sacred shrine
To shield their hearts and raise their spirits
Each time they fall? But why be faint
When courage carries all before it!

Another gust of wind. LUCIFER *appears before the terrified pair.*
The sky darkens. LUCIFER *laughs*

Why stare?

To EVE, *who is about to flee*

Ah lovely lady, wait!
A moment I beg to marvel at you.

EVE *stops and slowly plucks up courage*

LUCIFER
aside

A pretty pattern of perfections.

Aloud

Frightened, Adam?

ADAM

Of you, low creature?

LUCIFER
aside

A father fit to sire proud men.

Aloud

Greetings to you, brother spirit!

ADAM

Who are you, tell me?
From worlds below ours or above?

LUCIFER

Precisely as you please, to us
There is no difference in degree.

ADAM

I did not know that other men could be.

LUCIFER

But there is so much more you do not know
And never will. Do you suppose
The Ancient in simplicity

Created you from dust that you
Might share His world? You give Him praise:
He keeps you well supplied in turn.
He says to you, Take this, Leave that,
And tends and leads you like a sheep;
You have no need for wit at all.

ADAM

For wit? Do I not have my wits?
Do I not feel the blessed daylight,
The sweet delight of being alive,
The endless goodness of my God
Who placed me here as the world's prince?

LUCIFER

The tiny maggot, who consumes
The fruit before you, thinks the same,
As does the eagle seizing on his prey.
What makes you nobler then than they?
One common spark burns in you all,
The stirring of one universal power;
Like individual ripples in a brook
You leap to light, then swiftly sink
Deep in your swart and common bed.
One thing only, the power of thought,
Which languishes in you, unwitting,
Might help you grow to proper manhood,
To trust in your own strength, to choose
Between the evil and the good,
To take charge of your destiny,
And free you from God's charity.
You might prefer to go on breeding
Like any worm in a warm dungheap,
Lapped within your feeble limits,
And waste your life in ignorance.
A satisfying faith is nice and neat:
It's nobler but harder to stand on your own feet.

ADAM

How you speak! it makes my head spin.

EVE

These beautiful new things you say inspire me.

LUCIFER

But knowledge alone is not enough;
For if it is to bear fruit in great deeds,
Eternal life is something else you need.
What can you do with this mere thimbleful?
These two trees here will make you lords of all,
The very two forbidden you
By God who first created you.
Taste this and you will equal God in wisdom,
Taste that, eternal youth and grace are yours.

EVE

How mean is our Master, after all!

ADAM

But what if you deceive us?

The heavens grow a little brighter

ANGELIC HOST

                    Alas, poor world,
The ancient spirit of denial tempts you.

THE VOICE OF THE LORD

Adam, take heed!

ADAM

What is that voice again?

LUCIFER

Only the wind shaking the branches.
   You elements,
   Lend aid, arise—
   Humanity
   Will be your prize.—

   A blast of wind. It grows darker

These two trees are mine!

ADAM

            But who, then, are you?
To all appearances you're just like us.

LUCIFER

See there, the eagle circling in the clouds;
And there the mole blindly turning the soil—
Each is bound by its own horizon.
The world of spirits lies beyond your sight,
And man appears to you the very peak
Of God's creation. Dogs seem so to dogs,
They favour you with their companionship.
But just as you despise the dog
And, like a god, control his fate
With here a curse and there a word of praise,
So we, proud natives of the realm
Of pure spirit, look down on you.

ADAM

And you are one of these pure spirits?

LUCIFER

Indeed I am, the mightiest of the mighty,
Who stood beside the throne of God
And had a portion of his great effulgence.

ADAM

Then why did you not stay in the bright heavens,
Why descend into this world of dust?

LUCIFER

I grew tired of second place,
Of life's unchanging ordered pace,
The piping choirs, their childish song
Of praise without a word of wrong.
I long for conflict and for strife
To bring new potent worlds to life
Where souls might grow in probity,
Where some brave souls might follow me.

ADAM

But God said He would punish us
If we should stray from our appointed path.

EVE

Why should he punish us? If He has set
The path we are to follow, surely He
Will have arranged that we can choose no other.
Why leave us standing above the deep,
Dizzy and abandoned to our doom?
Or if sin too is part of His design
As storms are of hot days,
Why blame the roll of thunder more
Than heat which gives us life?

LUCIFER

I see we have our first philosopher.
You are the first of many, my fair sister,
Who'll argue the same point a million ways.
A few of them will end their days in bedlam.
Others stop short, but none will find a refuge.
Do put aside this futile speculation,
There are so many fine shades of opinion
On every issue that if you try them all
You end up knowing less than when you started
Without a hope of reaching a conclusion.
Contemplation means the death of action.

EVE

In that case I will pluck the fruit.

ADAM

The Lord has put His curse on them.

LUCIFER *laughs*

                                        But pluck.
Whatever happens to us, let it happen.
Let us be wise, like God.

First EVE, *then* ADAM *taste of the apple*

EVE

                      Above all
Eternally young.

LUCIFER

This way, this way, quickly.

Here is the Tree of Eternal Life,
Now hurry!

He pulls them toward the other tree, but a CHERUB *with a flaming sword
bars their way*

CHERUB

Back with you, transgressors, back!

THE VOICE OF THE LORD

Adam, Adam, you have abandoned me
So I abandon you. Go, try your strength.

EVE

We're finished.

LUCIFER

You are discouraged?

ADAM

Not at all.
That shudder was my first awakening.
We're going, Eve. No matter where. Away!
This place already feels barren and strange.

ANGELIC HOST

Ah, weep for them, Angelic Host,
The lie prevails—the earth is lost.

SCENE 3

A landscape with palms, outside Eden. A small crude wooden hut. ADAM *is driving stakes into the ground to make a fence.* EVE *is building a bower.* LUCIFER *overlooks them.*

ADAM

So this is mine. The wide world is behind me.
This plot shall be my home. I'll master it,
Defend it from all harm of fowl or brute
And force the field to yield its fairest fruit.

EVE

And I will build a bower like that before
To conjure the Eden that is ours no more.

LUCIFER

What potent words are kin and property,
Like two great levers that shall move the world,
They will give birth to every pain and pleasure.
The two ideas will grow continuously,
Creating nations and industries,
Begetting greatness and nobility,
Devouring, in time, their own progeny.

ADAM

You speak in riddles. You promised wisdom—
I put aside instinctive joys,
Prepared to struggle, to be great. What for?

LUCIFER

You feel no different from before?

ADAM

I feel that when the Lord abandoned me
And thrust me into the desert, empty handed,
I too abandoned him. My God is me,
Whatever I regain is mine by right.
This is the source of all my strength and pride.

LUCIFER
aside

Thumb your nose at heaven, vain puppet, you!
We'll see your mettle when storms buffet you.

EVE

My only source of pride is to know
That I shall be the mother of the world.

LUCIFER
aside

What fine ideals fill her heart. To be
The carrier of sin and misery.

ADAM

What should I thank Him for? This mere existence?
If mere existence can be justified
The fruits of my exertions must suffice.
In order to take pleasure in plain water
I have to work and feel my thirst the keener.
Each honeyed kiss untunes us, the price of that
Is what it brings in tow: it leaves us flat.
But though the bonds of gratitude have snapped
And fallen from me, and though I am free
To reconstruct my fate or wreck it again,
Stumbling in my efforts at perfection,

I doubt if help were needed to get this far,
To do this much was quite within my power.
You haven't freed me from the heavy chains
That bind my mortal body to the dust.
I feel entwined by something I can't name,
One hair, or something frailer, to my shame,
A curb on my ambitious spirit. Look,
I try to leap: my body drags me down,
My eyes and ears refuse to serve me when
I would be prying into hidden knowledge,
And even when imagination raises me
Mere hunger plucks me down and humbles me,
And makes me descend once more into base matter.

LUCIFER

That single strand has greater strength than I have.

ADAM

You must be weak indeed to be defeated
By this invisible web, this piece of nothing
Among whose strands a million creatures feel
At liberty to frolic as they please,
Whose presence is suspected by no more
Than a few exalted spirits at the most.

LUCIFER

It is the only thing that can defy me,
Because, like me, it is pure spirit. You think
It frail because it seems to work obscurely?
Not in the least: it sits and waits in darkness,
Creating or destroying galaxies.
Your head would spin if you could see it plain.
Man's work alone depends on sound and fury
And that can be contained in a mere thimble.

ADAM

You know how strong I am, so let me see—
A glimpse is all I want—that mechanism
Which so effects me, though I am expressly
Designed for self-sufficiency.

LUCIFER

"I am"—what foolish words! You were, you will be.
All life is an eternal ebb and flow.
But go on, look, my spirits will lend you eyes.

ADAM
who, as he speaks, begins to see what he describes

What flood is boiling up and rising
Ever higher all about me,
Dividing into two and rumbling
Like thunder towards the Poles?

LUCIFER

Heat quickening a land of ice.

ADAM

And those two streams of fire roaring
And racing beside me, I fear they'll sweep me away
Although I feel their generative power.

LUCIFER

Magnetism. Fields of force.

ADAM

The earth is shaking. What seemed firm and boundless
Is seething matter, irresistibly
Striving for form, struggling to be born.
See, here it shapes a flower, there a crystal.
But in all this wild confusion what becomes
Of me, of my self-image, of that body
In which I fondly trusted, like a child,
Imagining it was a worthy tool
To help me gain my ends and my desires?
Spoilt infant, pampered brat, who brings me pain
And pleasure, indiscriminate in both,
Are you to be reduced to a few handfuls
Of fine dust, a residue of water
And thin air? So radiant and glowing
Even now, are you to dissolve in clouds?
Each word I speak, each thought I form, consumes
My being drop by drop. I burn away!
Perhaps some hidden and mysterious spirit
Fans these fearsome flames, hoping to warm
Himself beside my ashes. Take it away!
Oh take away this dream which drives me mad.
It is terrible to stand alone among
A hundred warring elements and feel
That sense of sharp and utter desolation!
O why did I dismiss that providence
I felt instinctively but could not prize.
My intellect now yearns in vain for it.

EVE

Yes, yes, I too feel the same.
While you are striving against beasts of prey
And I am wearily toiling in the garden,
I look about me, searching the horizon,
But neither on earth nor in heaven do I see
A single friend to cheer or comfort me.
How different it was in the good old days.

LUCIFER
mocking

Well then, if you're both so feeble minded
That you catch cold without a nurse or mother,
And if you must serve someone,
I'll summon up a god to suit your needs,
Someone nicer than old Nobodaddy:
The Spirit of the Earth, a decent lad—
I used to know him in the Heavenly Choir.
    Spirit, no one else would dare
    To summon from the Earth, appear!
    The Spirit of Denial's voice
    Takes no deny and leaves no choice.

*Flames shoot from the ground, a thick black cloud appears with a rainbow,
rolling with thunder*

LUCIFER
stepping back

Who are you, Terror? I did not call you.
The Spirit of the Earth is meek and mild.

SPIRIT OF THE EARTH

What in the Heavenly Choir seemed weak to you
Is infinite and strong in its own sphere—
Now here I am because I must obey
The words of spirits, but take note of this:
To rouse is one thing, to control another.
My true form is too harsh a sight for you—
And as for these two worms, it would destroy them.

LUCIFER

Inform me then, if man would worship you
And make you his god, how may he approach you?

SPIRIT

Dispersed among the waters and the clouds,
In groves, in every place that man surveys
With strong desire and elevated spirits.

The SPIRIT *disappears. The springs and groves are peopled with playful*
nymphs

EVE

Ah look at those sweet kindred faces,
Look, just look, how charmingly they greet us,
Now farewell wilderness and desolation,
True happiness has come to dwell among us.
They'll comfort us when we are low
And give us good advice when we're in doubt.

LUCIFER

Nor could you wish for better counsellors,
Since by the time you ask you have decided—
And these delightful evanescent creatures
Will answer in the spirit of the question.
They smile benignly on the pure in heart
But seem horrendous to the desperate,
They'll company you in a myriad shapes,
A hundred transformations, till you die.
They offer cooling shade to fevered minds,
Ideals to the eternal young-in-heart.

ADAM

What's that to me? What is this mirage,
This glittering display I cannot grasp?
To me it's yet another mystery.
Don't monkey with me, Lucifer. Enough!
Where is the knowledge that you promised me?

LUCIFER
aside

Bitter enough will it seem in time to come—
You'll wish for ignorance before we're through.

aloud

Have patience please. You know you have to struggle
To earn even your momentary pleasures.
You have so much to learn yet. Be prepared
For many disappointments on the way.

ADAM

It's easy enough for you to talk of patience—
Eternity's vast store is laid before you.
But I've not tasted of the Tree of Life;
A thimbleful of time means I must hurry.

LUCIFER

All creatures have an equal share in time,
The hundred year old tree, ephemeral flies,
All feel, take pleasure, propagate and die
Having fulfilled their needs, used up their day.
It is not time that moves, but we who change.
A century, a day—it makes no difference.
So never fear, you too will run your race,
But do not think that man's entire self
Is bound up with this lump of clay, the body.
You've seen the anthill, no doubt, and the beehive:
A thousand workers stumbling to and fro,
Unconsciously they do, they err, they die.
The organism though, the One, lives on
By instinct shaped into a single mass,
Fulfilling its delineated purpose
Until the day when everything must end.
You too will come to dust, it is quite true,
But in a hundred forms you'll live again

And never will you have to start afresh
Since when you err, your son will bear the blame,
You pass on to him your feebleness, your gout—
All that you feel, experience and learn
Remains your own throughout a million years.

ADAM

This backward glance might satisfy an old man:
My heart is young, its passions are quite different.
I want to see the future, to discover
What I must struggle for, what I must suffer.
Let me see too, if I am to retain
My charm through all the changes that remain.

LUCIFER

So let it be. I'll cast a spell on you
And you will see unto the end of time
As in a dream, in fleeting images.
But when you see how foolish are your aims,
How fierce the war in which you are engaged,
I'll grant you—to prevent you from despair
And to maintain your courage in the battle—
A tiny ray of light there in the sky,
That you might think the whole dream was a mirage.
That tiny ray of light will be called Hope.

LUCIFER *leads* ADAM *and* EVE *into the hut. They fall asleep.*

SCENE 4

In Egypt. Before an open hall. ADAM, *as a youthful* PHARAOH, *seated on a throne.* LUCIFER *is his minister. A magnificent retinue attends at a respectable distance. In the background, slaves are building a pyramid driven on by guards with whips. Clear daylight.*

LUCIFER

My lord, your subjects who would gladly shed
Their life-blood for you are concerned to know
What prevents great Pharaoh from enjoying
Tranquil rest upon his pillowed throne?
Why renounce, they ask, the joys of daylight,
The charming dreams and images of night,
Why not instead allow some useful slave
To bear the burden of your grand design,
Since every honour, every potency
The world can offer is already yours,
As well as all the pleasures man can bear.
A hundred rich dominions call you master,
For you their flowers offer up their fragrance,
For you alone the sweet fruit grows and ripens,
It is for you a thousand women sigh,
The flaxen beauty with her languid eyes,
So delicate and fair, a vision dancing,
The girl with auburn hair and panting lips,
Whose burning eyes are maddened with desire—
All yours, my lord. Your whims dictate their fate,
And each of them will feel herself fulfilled
If she may tender you a moment's pleasure.

ADAM

Not one of these things takes my fancy now,
They are my due, like taxes. I don't earn them
Through my own exertions or in heat of battle.—
But with this work which occupies me now

I do believe I've found the way to greatness.
Nature herself will wonder at such skill,
And ring my name down the millennia.
Earthquake or tempest—nothing can destroy it.
Man has become more powerful than God.

LUCIFER

But Pharaoh, lay your hand upon your heart
And tell me if this prospect makes you happy.

ADAM

Ah no, there is an untold emptiness,
Some awful void. No matter, it is glory
I want, not happiness. And glory waits.
If only they knew nothing of my sorrow:
The masses cease to worship when they pity.

LUCIFER

But what if one day you should see through glory
And find it a mere transitory plaything.

ADAM

Impossible!

LUCIFER

But all the same.

ADAM

                I'd die
And curse the world to come.

LUCIFER

You will see through it,
But you'll not die—in fact you'll start upon
A fresh career. With much the same success.

The overseers beat one of the SLAVES *so fiercely that he runs in anguish
into the hall and falls before the throne*

SLAVE

My lord, your help!

EVE, *as his bride, rushes forward from the ranks of the workers and
embraces her husband, weeping passionately*

EVE

It's no use asking him.
How could one who has never felt our pain
Begin to understand it. The higher the throne
The fainter sounds the cry. Why not call me?
My body covers yours and takes the force
Of every blow.

ADAM

to the overseers who crowd forward to take the pair away

Leave her. Off with you!

They go

What strange emotion flutters at my heart?
Who is this woman, and what kind of charm
Does she possess that she can drag great Pharaoh
Down to the dust beside her with its chains?

He rises

LUCIFER

Another piece of webbing, that is all,
Which God, in mockery, has wound about you,
So that, when in your vanity, you play
At butterflies, you'll not forget that you
Were once a grub. You saw before how strong
This slender thread can be, which slips through fingers
So I cannot tear it.

ADAM
descending from the throne

                    Do not even try to.
It is as comforting as it is galling.

LUCIFER

Philosophers and kings, however, should not
Toil within its webs.

ADAM

                    Then what am I to do?

LUCIFER
mocking

There's nothing for it but for science to
Deny that such a hidden thread exists.
Let energy and matter scoff at it.

ADAM

But I can neither scoff at it nor deny it.

EVE

Ah dearest, how you bleed! I'll staunch the flow.
Your suffering must be unbearable.

SLAVE

What hurts is life. Its pain is quickly over.

EVE

You must not say that! Why live just so long
To die but now when we have found each other?

SLAVE

A slave? Why does he live—to carry stones
And raise his master's pyramid, to breed
His own successor for the yoke, and die.
A million souls for one.

ADAM

     What awful words,
Oh Lucifer!

LUCIFER

  The babbling of a corpse.

ADAM

What was he saying?

LUCIFER

    Why should you care, Pharaoh?
It is, indeed, a most important matter
To see the rank of slaves reduced by one.

EVE

Only a sum to you, the world to me.
Merciful heavens, who will love me now?

SLAVE

Not I, no longer—you must forget me, woman.

He dies

ADAM

Then I will love you. Take away the body.

They raise the body

Arise, madam, your place is on the throne
Upon the cushion. You are the paragon
Of beauty and I of power. We are fated
To meet each other everywhere.

EVE

                Your highness,
I know too well that you command the fate
Of slaves. I do not question it. But wait—
Give me a little time, then I am yours.

ADAM

No, not that word again. Is everything
To come to me through that one word 'command'?

EVE

Oh let it be enough that your command
Does not distress me—and do not be jealous
Of tears that I must shed for one who is dead.
How fair he is in death. My Lord, how fair!

She flings herself across the corpse

ADAM

Both fair and dead: how strange a contradiction.
Such stillness mocks at our ambition, smiles
With pity at our vanity.

LUCIFER

A slave,
One who escaped you, mocks at you and says,
My strength is greater now than all your fetters.

ADAM

Peace to the dead and greetings to the living.
He cannot feel your tears, but oh I suffer
Agonies without your smile.

They take the dead man out. ADAM *leads* EVE *to the throne*

Come here.
How sweet to lay my head against your breast.

A cry of pain from among the workers. EVE *shudders*

ADAM

What is it, my love?

EVE

Oh can't you hear
The people's cry of pain?

ADAM

It is the first time
I have noticed it. A sorry music—
But come and kiss me and forget the world.

To Lucifer

And you, please put an end to all this wailing.

LUCIFER

I can't do that. It is the people's birthright,
One that they inherit with the yoke.

Another cry of pain. EVE *screams out.* ADAM *rises*

ADAM

Oh lady, you are suffering and I
Hardly know how to help you. That cry, like lightning,
Pierces your heart and strikes at my head. It feels
As if the world were crying out for help.

EVE

Oh Pharaoh, crush me if you will—forgive me
If the people's cry of woe won't let me rest.
I am your slave, as I know very well,
My life's one purpose is to give you pleasure.
I will forget about the world outside:
The splendour, poverty, the dreams, the dead,
I'll sweeten my smile and make my lips more luscious.
But when the people, that million-limbed creature
Begins to moan under the lash, then I,
Their exiled daughter, and a tiny part
Of that great aching body, feel each cry
Of every pain they suffer in my heart.

ADAM

I feel with you—a million souls for one—
The dead man's words...

EVE

                        You are melancholy,
Great Pharaoh. It is my fault. Drive me off
Or teach me to be deaf.

ADAM

You'd make a finer tutor
For you can teach me how to hear such pain.
I've had enough. Oh, liberate the slaves,
Dismiss them all. What is the point of glory
If it can only be achieved through torture,
Through one man sacrificing millions
In whom there breathes the same clear human spirit?
I feel a million pains for each delight.

LUCIFER

Pharaoh, you are confused. The masses are
Mere creatures of fate, living under sentence.
You'd see them tread the mill in any system,
That is what they are made for. Free them now
And they'd gain nothing by your futile gesture—
Tomorrow they would seek another master.
Do you imagine you could sit astride them
Were they themselves not anxious to have masters?
If there were any consciousness in them?

ADAM

But why this wailing—could it be the yoke
Tormented them?

LUCIFER

Something hurts them, true,
But what, they could not tell you. Men seek power
And that is all there is. It is the spur.
It's not fraternity that drives the masses
Towards the flag of freedom. I do not say
That they would recognize this—no; they itch
For novelty and spurn a settled order;
They hope to realize in novelty
Their dreams of happiness. An unplumbed sea

The people: sunbeams cannot penetrate
Their murky depths. But one wave scintillates,
A single fleeting brilliance. A wave like you.

ADAM

Why me?

LUCIFER

　　　　Or someone like you. One in whom
The people's instinct comes to consciousness,
Some venerated champion of freedom
Who dares to oust you from your shining realm.
The masses, of course, never profit by it:
The names may change, the master still remains.

ADAM

Your logic runs in never ending circles
From which there seems no prospect of escape.

LUCIFER

Escape there is. Present a chosen few
With necklaces or rings or some such bauble,
And say to them: I raise you from the crowd,
You are hereby ennobled—they'll believe you,
And looking down on others with disdain
Accept, without demur, your condescension.

ADAM

Please spare me all your specious arguments.
Away with slavery, let them all go free.
Inform them of this now, with greatest haste,
Immediately, before I change my mind.

LUCIFER
aside

Proceed with all your vanity, be gone:
You think you act—it's fate that draws you on.

He leaves

ADAM

The work must stop, unfinished as it is,
The fragments will serve to humble the ambitious,
A paradox of power and impotence.

Great joy outside as the workers disperse. LUCIFER *returns*

Rejoice, you slaves, your lord bows down before you.
But never think he was compelled to it.

EVE

Console yourself, my love, for after all
What earthly use are pomp and circumstance?
They creep and crawl between us like a snake.

ADAM

How vast, how vast it is!

EVE

Away with it.
You see, the cries have stopped. Our courting will
Be undisturbed. Oh lean against my bosom—
What more can you desire?

ADAM

How restricted
Are your horizons, woman. And yet this
Precisely is what charms ambitious men—

The strong are fated to desire the weak.
It's what a parent feels so ardently
When holding his helpless child within his arms.

EVE

Perhaps, O Pharaoh, I already bore you
With needless, incoherent chattering.
I cannot help it if I am no wiser.

ADAM

Do not even wish to be, my dearest.
One intellect is quite enough for me.
It's not for power or majesty I seek
Your breast, nor knowledge. Books can grant me these
More readily. Simply continue talking,
Talk on, that I may ever hear your voice,
Suffuse my heart with its sweet resonance,
Say anything whatever. Oh, who wants
To know what little birds are singing when
They bring such intimations of delight.
Be but a flower, be charming bric-a-brac
Whose worth lies not in function but sheer beauty.

To Lucifer

But something bothers me and breaks the spell
Of sensuous reverie. It may be foolish
And yet, I beg you, satisfy this longing—
Let me cast just one intrepid glance
Into the future, a few millennia hence,
And know my reputation.

LUCIFER

                    Can you feel,
Even as you kiss, a light caressing
Breeze that touches your face, then flies away?
It leaves the faintest coating of fine dust.

Next year you'll see it gathering in creases,
A century, you plunge your arm in it;
A thousand years, your pyramids are buried;
Great drifts of sand obliterate your name;
Your pleasure gardens fill with cries of jackals;
A race of slaves and beggars roam the desert.

All that LUCIFER *describes becomes visible*

No fearful cataclysm brings this on,
No thunderstorms or earthquakes are required;
A breeze, that's all, the breeze which plays about you.

ADAM

A dreadful sight!

LUCIFER
mocking

Why worry? It is only
Your soul that's lost, your body stays intact
And perfectly preserved for curious schoolboys
To puzzle at your twisted face, to guess
From scuffed inscriptions if you're slave or master?

He kicks at a mummy which has appeared before the throne.
It rolls down the stairs

ADAM
leaping up

Infernal image! Get away from me!
Vain strife and even emptier ambition—
A million souls for one—the words still ring.
And so I must emancipate the millions
In one free state. There's nothing left for it.
Let one man die providing the state lives
And makes an entity of single men.

Eve

And will you leave me too, your own true love?

Adam

Yes—you, the throne, I must leave everything.
Lead on, O Lucifer, to some new goal.
I've wasted too much time in this blind alley.

He sets out with drawn sword

Eve

My lord, remember—if you should return
With shattered hopes, my heart will offer shelter.

Adam

Indeed, I think I will discover you
In purer form wherever we next meet,
But then you will embrace me not as slave
But as an equal with a sense of pleasure.

He goes

Lucifer

Why all this haste? You'll get there soon enough,
Sooner perhaps than you had hoped. Your folly
Will find you out and leave you melancholy.
It should be most amusing. Let's be off.

SCENE 5

*Athens. A public square with a tribune in the centre. On one side, in the fore-
ground, the open porch of a temple with statues of gods, garlands and an altar.
Eve as Lucia, wife of Miltiades the general (Adam), with her son Kimon, is
accompanied by a few slaves bearing objects for sacrifice. She approaches the
temple. A sunny morning. Ragged people are moving to and fro.*

EVE

This way, dear son, this way. Now look out there—
You father's nimble craft took just that course,
Bound for a war beyond our own frontiers.
Barbarians live there, a reckless people,
Threatening our country's liberty.
Pray, pray, my son, that heaven defend our cause
And bring your noble father safely home.

KIMON

But why should father travel all that way
To defend such cowardly and ragged people,
Leaving you, dear mother, to pine at home?

EVE

Hush! You must not judge your virtuous father—
The curse of heaven lies on such a child.
Only a doting woman has the right
To rue the greater actions of her husband
Which, were he to neglect, might bring disgrace.
Your father acted as becomes a man.

KIMON

You fear he's weak, and might be beaten, mother?

EVE

Oh no, my son, your father's brave, he'll triumph.
There's only one thing that I am afraid of,
That he may fail to conquer himself.

KIMON

But how?

EVE

In the human soul there dwells a powerful voice—
Ambition is its name. In slaves it's dormant
Or else, for lack of scope, turns criminal.
But liberty enriches it with blood,
And it expands, attains to civic virtue
Which in its turn gives birth to all things sweet
And noble. Grown overweening though it turns
Against its mother, until one or the other
Bleeds to death. Should this voice strengthen in him
So he betrayed his sacred home, then I,
Yes, even I would curse him. Pray, my son.

They enter the temple. More people collect in the precinct

FIRST MAN

We never hear exciting news these days,
It seems our troops have failed to find the enemy.

SECOND MAN

And here at home the world has grown so sleepy,
Old habits of intrigue are quite neglected—
To put one into execution would
Give people's throats at least some exercise.
All morning I've been up and down the agora
But nobody has tried to buy my vote.

FIRST MAN

A dull old life, but what are we to do?

THIRD MAN

A little stirring would not come amiss.

EVE *in the meantime has lit the altar fire, washed her hands, and prepared her sacrifice. Her attendants begin a chant which, verse by verse, blends into the next scene. The place is now filled with people. Two* DEMAGOGUES *contest the podium*

FIRST DEMAGOGUE

Get off. This pitch is mine. If I don't speak
Our country's threatened and might well be lost.

The people roar approval

SECOND DEMAGOGUE

It's lost each time you do. Get off, you hireling!

The people laugh and applaud

FIRST DEMAGOGUE

But you're no hireling—nobody would hire you!
Dear citizens, it is with pain I speak,
Because it hurts a noble heart to bring
The mighty down to earth; and I must now
Drag one such man from his triumphal car
To face your judgment.

SECOND DEMAGOGUE

              Well begun, you schemer.
Yes, deck the sacrificial beast with garlands
Before you lead him to the block.

First Demagogue

Get off!

The People

Why should we listen to this renegade?

They begin to tug at the Second Demagogue

First Demagogue

However it may hurt me, I must speak,
Because, O noble and all-powerful people
I prize you above any general.

Second Demagogue

This treacherous and undernourished rabble,
These dogs who lick scraps from their master's table?
You craven coward, I don't envy your taste.

The People

Down with him, the traitor, down with him.

They treat him even more roughly. Eve *sacrifices two doves and throws incense on the altar*

Eve

O Holy Aphrodite, please accept
This smoke of sacrifice and hear my prayer.
I do not plead for laurel leaves to bless
My husband's brow, but that his conquering breast
Might feel the warmth of homely tenderness.

A smiling Eros *appears in the smoke of the sacrifice, surrounded by* Graces *who cast rose petals over him. The group stands in deep devotion*

ATTENDANTS

O hear her prayer!

EROS

A pure heart's benediction
On you, woman.

GRACES

And the protection of the Graces.

ATTENDANTS

All hail, Aphrodite!

FIRST DEMAGOGUE

Hear my charge,
O people! Great Miltiades betrays
The country.

SECOND DEMAGOGUE

He is lying! He is lying!
Hear me out now, or later bear the shame
Of your remorse.

FIRST MAN

Get down from there, you scoundrel!

He is swept away into the crowd

FIRST DEMAGOGUE

The flower of our youth is in his hands.
Lemnos he took at one fell swoop, but now
He loiters at Pharos. He has been bought off.

THIRD MAN

He must be killed!

FIRST CITIZEN

That's right, let's hear your voice
Or else be off with you, and off my payroll.

The sacrifice is over, the gods are gone

EVE
rising

What is that noise outside? Let's see, my son.

KIMON

It is a traitor they're condemning, mother.

EVE
moving to the top of the steps

My heart quakes when I see a hungry people
Passing judgment on the high and mighty.
When the illustrious are dragged through mud
The mob looks on and gloats maliciously,
As if this somehow justified their filth.

SECOND MAN

My lord, I'd like to shout, but I am hoarse.

SECOND CITIZEN

Here you are, go lubricate your throat.

SECOND MAN

What should I cry?

SECOND CITIZEN

Demand the fellow's death.

THE PEOPLE

Kill him! Kill him!

EVE

Who are they baying for?

SECOND DEMAGOGUE
moving to her

Who else but him who towers a head above
His fellow men—something they can't bear.

EVE

Miltiades? Great heavens! And you too,
Old Crispus, you who were a slave until
My husband freed you, you call for his death?

CRISPUS

Forgive me, lady, only one of us
May live. My paymaster helps to maintain
My children, three of them.

EVE

Alas, poor Crispus,
That fate should so degrade you. If you're starving
I forgive you. But as for you, Thersites,
And for the rest of you who snoozed away
Your comfortable lives, without a care,
While he, my husband, beat back enemies
Outside the gate.—Oh, you ungrateful people!

THERSITES

It is indeed a bitter blow, my lady,
But what can we do in the current mood:
And who would dare to stake his whole estate
Against such scum, so hot with agitation!

FIRST DEMAGOGUE

I now pronounce the judgment of the people.

LUCIFER *runs on in the guise of a terrified soldier*

LUCIFER

I bring you news of danger. The enemy
Is at the gates!

FIRST DEMAGOGUE

Impossible! Is not
Our victorious commander at the head?

LUCIFER

Yes, the foe himself. He heard you plotting,
And in his heart there rose a righteous anger.
It's the fire and the sword for you this time.

SECOND DEMAGOGUE

You traitors, you have brought all this on us!

THE PEOPLE

Destroy them now—hurrah for the commander!
God help us all, let's run wherever we can.
The end is here!

FIRST DEMAGOGUE

No. Get before the gates
And render him homage!

EVE

Now, by all the gods!
The judgment hurt me when I lost you through it,
But though this reunites us, my dear husband,
How much the worse to know it was deserved.

FIRST MAN

Take the man's wife: if the city comes to harm
We'll execute the pair, both child and mother.

EVE

I'd be happy enough to die for you, dear husband,
But let the child escape this country's curse.

KIMON

Have no fear for me, mother, come with me.
This holy place will shield us from assault.

They step into the temple where two nymphs lower rose garlands behind
them to keep the people out, who immediately withdraw. Off stage the
sound of trumpets. People scatter screaming. The nymphs too disappear

LUCIFER
cackling and rubbing his hands

A delicious joke. Pure intellect finds all
Scenes of heartbreak immensely comical.

Facing the temple

If only the sight of this eternally
Refreshed and youthful beauty did not shake me,
Oh what a chill this strange power wakes in me
That lends a naked body modesty,
Ennobles sin and renders fate sublime
Covering it with roses and sweet kisses
Of simplicity. But why this long delay
Before my world with all its monstrous forms,
Of terror and uncertainty, can come
Into its own and frighten off this mirage,
Which reawakens humankind each time
I sense the victory at hand. But wait,
And we shall see when death in all its horror
Makes its appearance in a little while
Whether this poor shadow play has run
Its course and finally rung down the curtain.

He blends into the crowd.
ADAM, *in the guise of wounded* MILTIADES, *leads an armed company into the forum. The* DEMAGOGUES *and the crowd go pleading before him*

THE PEOPLE

Long live the leader! Pardon us, my lord!

ADAM

What have you done that you should beg my pardon?
What can the strong require from the weak?
But where's my wife to greet me, and my child—
Surely no harm can have befallen them?

EVE

O why return at all, Miltiades,
If I can take no pleasure in your coming?
My son, support your mother or she faints…
He leaves you nothing, not even his honour!

ADAM

What is this? I don't understand. The people
Crawl before me, my own wife curses me
And all the while my wounds bleed for my country.

EVE

Your country and my heart both bleed the more.
Why come trailing battalions behind you?

ADAM

Is this so unbefitting to my rank?
I come because a serious wound prevents me
From exercising all my usual duties.
I come to lay my power before the feet
Of my commissioners, the mighty people,
To render up to them my true account.
You are discharged, my honourable fellows,
You've earned the sanctuary of hearth and home.
And as for me, I dedicate to thee,
Pallas Athene, my sword upon thine altar.

He is helped into the temple. His troops disperse

EVE
embracing him

Miltiades, you great and noble man,
Show me a happier woman than your wife!
Look, look—your son, how he resembles you,
How tall he is, how handsome!

ADAM

                    Ah, my dears!

KIMON

Of course I knew whatever father did
Was sure to be done well.—

EVE

                  Oh do not shame me,
I should have known it better, being his wife.

ADAM

My son, present your father's sword for him.

KIMON
hanging up the sword

Take charge, O Goddess, of this precious sword
Until the time when I return for it.

EVE

This double sacrifice may I, as mother,
Strew with incense. Observe it, O Athene.

She sprinkles incense

FIRST DEMAGOGUE
on the rostrum

Was I not right to say he was a traitor?
That Darius bribed him? The wound was a mere sham.
He simply does not wish to fight in battle.

THE PEOPLE

Then he must die!

ADAM

What is that noise outside?

EVE

Such dreadful words, Miltiades. The mob—
They still insist on calling you a traitor.

ADAM

Ridiculous! That I who gained the victory
At Marathon should now be called a traitor.

EVE

How true! The world has grown so wicked in your
Absence.

FIRST DEMAGOGUE

Why wait? Take him!

The people crowd before the temple, LUCIFER *among them*

EVE

           Miltiades!
This sanctuary will shield us, stay in there.—
Oh, why did you dispense with all your troops?
And why did you not sack this den of vice?
These guttersnipes are only fit for shackles;
They realize that you were born to rule them,
Are nobler than the lot of them together,
And that is why they'd sooner murder you
Than worship at your feet.

FIRST DEMAGOGUE

              You hear her words?
A traitor's wife!

EVE

                It is a woman's right
To shield her husband even if he is guilty,
Then how much more when he is innocent
As my lord is, and his foes as foul as you.

FIRST DEMAGOGUE

O mighty populace! Why let yourself
Be so insulted by her?

FIRST MAN

                Perhaps she's right.

FIRST CITIZEN

Whoever speaks for them is suspect. Bawl
Your filthy lungs out or you'll starve like beasts.

THE PEOPLE

Kill him! Kill him!

ADAM

                Shield the boy, don't let him
See my blood. Don't cling to my breast, woman.
The lightning that's about to strike the rock
Must not strike you. Now let me die alone—
Why strive to live when the idea of freedom
For which I always fought appears so senseless.

FIRST DEMAGOGUE

Why hesitate?

The People

Let's kill him. Kill him now!

Adam

I cannot bring myself to curse this rabble,
They're not to blame, they were created craven.
Sheer misery has marked them down as slaves,
And slavery degrades them to this level—
The bloody tools of puffed-up demagogues.
And only I was fool enough to think
That people such as this would welcome freedom.

Lucifer
aside

The perfect epitaph! And it will do
For the tombs of many great men after you.

Adam

Take me away. I make no further claim
Upon this sanctuary.

He allows himself to be taken away down the stairs, giving Eve *tenderly
over to the care of her attendants*

I am ready now.

Second Demagogue

Defend yourself. Not everything is lost.

Adam

This injury would cry out if I spoke
In my defence.

Second Demagogue

But speak. These very people
Grovelled before you just a while ago.

Adam

That is why it's useless. They won't forgive
The victim of their own depravity.

Lucifer

Then you are disillusioned?

Adam

Yes, immensely.

Lucifer

And you admit you were a nobler master
To foolish crowds like this than they to you?

Adam

Quite possibly, but both are damnable:
The names have changed, the outcome is the same.
How vain to fight against it. From now on
I shall not even try, since after all
What is there for fervent hearts to strive for?
No, let them live entirely for pleasure
And fill their thimbleful of life with it,
Then they can stagger drunkenly to Hades.
Show me a new path, Lucifer. Lead on,
And I will shake with laughter at all virtue
And all suffering. Give me the sensual life.
And you, O woman, you, who I recall
Once conjured me a bower in the desert,
If you bring up my son a citizen
As honest mothers do, then you are mad.

The painted girl who sits in the bordello
With puckered lips, her passions roused by wine,
Is right to mock you. Laugh—deny your virtue.
And now the bloody scaffold for my sins,
Though not for petty crime but something graver,
For inspiration by a noble cause.

In the meantime a block is brought before the temple steps. LUCIFER *stands
beside it with an axe.* ADAM *bows his head*

FIRST DEMAGOGUE

Deliver the blow, and long live our great country!

LUCIFER
whispering to ADAM

A pretty farewell, don't you think? And now
My noble sir, do you not feel the chill,
The shudder as that ugly creature Death
Blows ever nearer with his icy breath?

EVE

Pallas, you did not hear my prayer!—

From the temple issues the GENIUS OF DEATH *in the guise of a mild
looking youth. He approaches* ADAM *with a flaming torch held upside
down, and a wreath*

ADAM

                            She heard,—
Athene listened. Heaven will protect you.
Now suddenly my heart is calm, Lucia.

LUCIFER

A curse on you, O world of vain illusions,
Once again you've ruined my finest moment.

EVE

I curse this nation, a cold and common crew!
For happiness unfitted by demeanour,
Her fresh blossoms lie withered at your feet,
Although your freedom may seem sweet to you,
The bitterness for me is much the keener.

SCENE 6

Rome. An open porch with statues of the gods, vessels with incense, a view of the Apennines. In the centre a table is spread with three couches round it. ADAM is SERGIOLUS, LUCIFER is MILO. Also present are CATULUS and other revellers. EVE is JULIA who, together with HIPPIA and CLUVIA, other ladies of pleasure, is appropriately clad and enjoying herself. There is a gladiatoral combat in progress on a raised platform. Slaves wait on the company, musicians play on flutes. It is dusk, deepening into night.

CATULUS

Look, Sergiolus, how lithe and skilful
That scarlet ribboned gladiator is.
I'll lay odds on the man to beat his rival.

ADAM

No, by Hercules.

CATULUS

By Hercules? But why?
Who here among us still believes in gods?
Swear by Julia, then I might believe you.

ADAM

By Julia then—

LUCIFER

Your vow has sure foundations:
Now one false idol makes way for another.
But how are we to understand this vow?
You swear by her beauty, by your love of her,
Or rather by her faithfulness to you?

CATULUS

All charm is transient—it therefore follows
What fascinates today is dull tomorrow,
A plainer woman will entice you from her
By force of her enchanting novelty.

ADAM

I meant her faithfulness. What man has squandered
More on his mistress than I on her?

HIPPIA

                              You clown,
You think you could remain entwined for ever?
And say it should be possible, could you,
Yes you,—insatiable in your desires,
Always flitting from woman to woman, finding
Some shred of pleasure in this one or the other,
All joy and beauty unattainably
And magically flitting for ever before you—
Could you be certain that some whim of hers,
One idle thought would not charm her away?
A gladiator's lacerated muscles...

ADAM

Yes, yes, you're right—but no more, Hippia.
Why Tantalus like, are we drawn to pleasures,
When we neither have the strength of Hercules,
Nor the Protean knack of changing shape,
And a wretched slave after a week of torture
Finds such enjoyment in one hour of freedom
His master vainly yearns for it. Is pleasure,
Like water, refreshment for the weary, but
Fatal to those who dive into its rapids?

LUCIFER

A splendid lecture on morality,
Spiced with wine and pillowed on soft breasts—
But as to your wager?—

ADAM

     If I should lose the bet
Then Julia is yours.

CATULUS

And if you win?

ADAM

Your horse is mine.

CATULUS

    You take her back next month,
And if you don't I'll throw her in my fishpond.

LUCIFER

Look, dear Julia, at this nice fat fish:
Eat up, eat up, you'll soon be food for others.

EVE

Will not this ugly maggot feast on you?
Whoever is alive let him rejoice,
And if he can't rejoice then let him laugh.

She drinks

ADAM

to the gladiator

Now mind to do your best!—

CATULUS

Fight like a soldier!

Catulus's gladiator falls, and begging for his life raises his fingers. ADAM wants to give him the sign of mercy but CATULUS holds his hand down and tightening his fist gives the gladiator the thumbs down

CATULUS

Recipe ferrum! Cowardly mongrel. I have
Sufficient slaves, I'm not a miser. Who,
Dear ladies, would begrudge you this excitement
When kisses taste so much the sweeter for it;
A little spilt blood sharpens our desire.

In the meantime the gladiator has been killed by his opponent

ADAM

The horse is mine. Come Julia, embrace me.
Kindly remove that corpse—and now, you dancers!
Perform some comic interlude for us,
We've had enough blood for today.

The corpse is removed and dancers occupy the platform

CATULUS

Come, Cluvia,
Come here to me. I can't look on for long
While others are embracing.

LUCIFER

And we, Hippia,
Should we follow their example, do you think?
First lick your lips, ensure they are not poisoned.
That's right. Now let's enjoy ourselves, my dear.

ADAM

Your heart is thumping so! What can it be?
I cannot rest, it beats so in my ear.

They whisper

LUCIFER

Hear the fool still blabbering of her 'heart'.

CATULUS

Look here, my sweet, I make no claim on yours,
Do with it what you like but don't tell me,
A good hot kiss will do for me quite nicely.

CLUVIA

How generous, darling! I raise my glass to you.

She drinks

CATULUS

That's good, dear Cluvia, but don't remove
Those tender arms and yielding little breasts.
Just look, my garland's slipping off my head.

To the dancers

Ah what a splendid pirouette that was,
Voluptuous fire and pleasure all combined!

CLUVIA

I don't like competition—if you talk
To them again I'll cover up your eyes.
I cannot squeeze a good word out of you.

Indicating LUCIFER

I'd rather you looked at that sour-faced wretch.
What good are girls to him, however pretty,
If he doesn't take the slightest notice of them
And leaves them snoring while he looks about him
With cold eyes and a supercilious smile
On the hundred sweet and idiotic things
That give our feast its flavour.

CATULUS

Indeed it is a face to throw a chill
Into a choir of poets. A man who resists
The spell of the moment and will not allow
His spirit to be swept off by the tide
Is good for nothing and should stay at home.

HIPPIA

To tell the truth I fear the poor man has
Contracted the Black Death which has destroyed
A good part of the city.

ADAM

     Away with all
This talk of gloom. A ribald song for us.
Whoever knows a good one, let us hear it.

HIPPIA
sings

A man can never have
Too much of wine or love;
Of wine there is profusion,
Each yields its flavour, thrives
On sweet intoxication,
Like sunlight on old graves
They gild our barren lives.
A man can never have
Too much of wine or love;
Of girls there is profusion,
Each casts her spell and thrives,

ALL

On sweet intoxication,
Like sunlight on old graves
They gild our barren lives.

CATULUS

Precisely so. Now Cluvia, your turn.

CLUVIA
sings

How foolish they were long ago:
When a handsome rogue laid low
Widowed Lucretia in her bed
Her lips were cold, her lust was dead,
No whoreson pleasure could she feel
But stuck herself instead with steel.

ALL

The world grows wiser by the minute,
Rejoice therefore that we live in it.

CLUVIA

How foolish they were long ago:
Poor Brutus from his house must go,
For arms his luxuries desert
And don the stinking trooper's shirt,
For ragged people give his blood
And perish duly in the mud.

ALL

The world grows wiser by the minute,
Rejoice therefore that we live in it.

CLUVIA

How foolish they were long ago:
Brave men perceive a spectral glow
And call it sacred. What a farce!
Were such a lunatic to pass
We could dependably rely on
Him to fatten the circus lion.

ALL

The world grows wiser by the minute,
Rejoice therefore that we live in it.

LUCIFER

Ah Cluvia, you've outsung Hippia.
I'd love to have composed that verse myself.

ADAM

Why are you moping, Julia? Why not sing?
Everybody else is in good spirits.
Don't you enjoy lying on my breast?

EVE

Oh certainly Sergiolus, and yet—
Such merriment has always left me serious.
I feel whatever laughs cannot be real.
The cup of happiness, however sweet,
Contains one drop of inexpressible pain.
Perhaps we apprehend such perfect moments
Are flowers, doomed to wither.

ADAM

I feel it too.

EVE

Especially when I hear songs and verses,
I am aware of more than words, but tides
That pulse beneath them, rocking like a boat—
I feel as if I lay within a dream:
The swaying sound brings back some distant past
When I was innocent and playful as a child
Under the palms, lost among the sunbeams,
Aware of noble voices in my soul.
Forgive me, this is nothing but the spell
Of silly dreams.—Kiss me again—I'm waking.

ADAM

No more of dancers or of songs. I'm sick
Of this eternal sea of sweetness. My heart
Requires something bitter for a change.
Some wormwood in my wine, a stinging lip,
A sense of danger hovering about me.

The dancers depart. A cry of pain outside

What is that cry that cuts me to the heart?

LUCIFER

They're crucifying a few lunatics
Who dream of justice and fraternity.

CATULUS

It serves them right—why can't they sit at home
Enjoying themselves and forget the world?
Why interfere in other people's business?

LUCIFER

The beggar wants the rich man for his brother,
But let them once change places and he'd do
His share of crucifying.

CATULUS

          Leave this subject—
We ought to laugh at misery and death,
At plagues which wreak such havoc in a town
And all those tricks of fate the gods dish out.

A new cry

ADAM
to himself

I feel as if I lay within a dream,
The swaying sound brings back a distant past...
Aware of noble voices in my soul...
Your very words, I think, my Julia?

EVE

          Yes.

It has grown dark in the meantime. A funeral procession with flutes,

torches and wailing women passes before the courtyard. The company falls
momentarily silent

LUCIFER
bursting into laughter

I see you've lost your humour in this gloom,
Have you run out of wine or lost your wit
That even sourpuss here has had enough?
One of us here is frightened, it appears,
Or else converted.

ADAM
throwing a glass at his head

Damn you if you think so!

LUCIFER

Wait! I'll invite a new guest to the party—
Perhaps he will revive your flagging spirits.
Look sharp, you slaves, and show the fellow in,
That man who travels by the light of torches—.
We only want to offer him a drink.

They bring in the corpse in an open coffin and put it on the table.
The mourners remain in the background. LUCIFER raises his glass
to the dead man

Drink up! To you today, to me tomorrow!

HIPPIA

Perhaps you would prefer a kiss?

LUCIFER

Embrace him.
I dare you to steal the obol from his mouth.

96

HIPPIA

If I can kiss you, dear, then why not him?

She kisses the corpse. St Peter *steps forward from the ranks
of the mourners*

St Peter

Stop it! You are sucking in the plague.

All recoil in horror and rise from their places

All

The plague! How horrible! Get rid of him!

St Peter

You wicked generation! Race of cowards
And tramplers upon virtue—mock at God!
While fortune smiles on you, you are like flies
Importunately buzzing in the sunlight,
But when some peril hammers at your door,
Or when God's mighty finger touches you
You shrink in fear and huddle in despair.
Do you not feel the weight of retribution
Across your back? But look, just look around you—
The city perishes and foreign hordes
Tread down your golden harvest. Rules of Law
Disintegrate, there's no commanding voice
And no-one listens. Robbery and murder
Are striding unashamed about your households,
On their heels follow grey anxiety
And terror. No help, no comfort, either
In earth or heaven. Will intoxication
Spirit away that deep sense of foreboding
That speaks within your heart and vainly urges

You to finer goals? For I hardly need
To add that satisfaction is beyond you,
That ecstasy awakes only disgust.
You look round terrified, with trembling lips,
But all in vain. Your faith in the old gods
Is quite exhausted. First they petrify
Then turn to dust,

> *The statues of the gods disintegrate*

           and no new idol comes
To raise them from the rubble. Look around you,
And see what wreaks more havoc in the town
Than pestilence, is mightier than the plague—
A thousand waken from soft pillows, seeking
The wilderness of Thebaïs in order
To populate it with a tribe of hermits
Endeavouring to find some new excitement,
Some keener stimulation for numbed senses—
Base generation! you shall pass away
In the vast purification of the world.

HIPPIA
collapsing before the table

Oh God have mercy! What dread agony,
Cold sweats and fires of Orcus—it's the plague,
The pestilence is on me—I am lost!
Oh will not one among you come to help me,
You with whom I shared my every pleasure?

LUCIFER

To you today, to me tomorrow, dearest.—

HIPPIA

In that case kill me or be cursed by me.

99

St Peter

stepping up to her

Forgive rather than curse him, O my daughter,
And I will help you, as will that great God,
The eternal God of blessed charity.
Aspire unto Him— with water now
I wash contamination from your soul,
And cleansed it flies to him.—

He baptizes her with water from a dish on the table

Hippia

Oh, father, I'm at peace.

She dies

Catulus

And I'll set out for Thebaïs today,
The corruption of the world disgusts me now.

Cluvia

Wait, Catulus, I am coming with you.

*They leave together. Adam, absorbed in thought, steps downstage,
followed by Eve*

Adam

Still here, my Julia? What can you want here
Where death has destroyed all forms of happiness?

Eve

Is not my place beside you, where you are?
Sergiolus, what wealth of noble feelings
Might you have found hidden in my bosom,
That bosom where you sought such fleeting pleasures?

ADAM

And in my own heart. A pity it is so.
What shame to die in misery and meanness,
Continually to suffer. If God lives,

He kneels and raises his hands to heaven

If He has but a thought for us and rules us,
Then let Him bring new people, new ideals
Into the world, and pour a finer blood
Into degenerate veins, that nobler men
May break the mould and strive beyond themselves
To higher things. Oh everywhere I feel
Such shabbiness, and we have no strength left
To start anew. O Lord, please hear my prayer!

The Cross, in a glory of light, appears in the sky.
Burning towns are glimpsed behind the mountains.
Barbarian tribes swarm down. A hymn is heard in the distance

LUCIFER
to himself

The sight sends a few shivers up my spine.
But is it not my task to strive with man?
Whatever I cannot perform he can.
I've witnessed similar capers in my time,
And once the glory fades and all is lost
There still remains behind the bloody Cross.

ST PETER

The Lord has hearkened to you. Look around—
Degenerate earth is straining for new birth.
These warriors, these savages in bearskin,
Who fling their brands against your shining cities,
Whose cavalry are tramping out the vintage
Of your past, who turn neglected temples
Into stables, they bring fresh stores of blood
To supplement your thin anaemic veins,

And those who in the circus chant their hymns
While ravening tigers tear out their intestines
Announce a new ideal of brotherhood,
The freedom of the individual soul.—
Ideas that roll like thunder through the world.

ADAM

I feel it, yes, I feel it. Soul disdains
Mere sluggish pleasures and soft counterpanes:
There is another pleasure set apart,
A joy in the slow draining of the heart.

ST PETER

So let it be your aim: to God the Glory,
To you the labour. The single soul is free
To bring to fullness all that lies within it.
And only one commandment binds it: Love.

ADAM

Rise, to battle, rise then in the fervour
Of new faith, and create another world
Of which the fair flower shall be chivalry,
Its altar poetry, and raised beside it
The high exalted feminine ideal.

He leans on ST PETER *and departs*

LUCIFER

How seemly for a man, how brave it is
To enthuse over impossibilities.
Such pious tendencies please the Creator,
And I'm in favour too—despair comes later.

He follows him

SCENE 7

Constantinople. Some CITIZENS *loitering in the market. In the centre, the Patriarch's palace, to the right a convent, to the left a grove.* ADAM *as* TANCRED *in the prime of manhood, with other knights, at the head of a troop of* CRUSADERS *returning from Asia. They wave flags and beat drums.* LUCIFER *is his esquire. Evening. Later night.*

FIRST CITIZEN

Here they come—a fresh host of barbarians!
Let's run and bar the entrances against them
In case they feel like robbing us again.

SECOND CITIZEN

Away with the women: these rough guttersnipes
Are familiar with the pleasures of the harem.

FIRST CITIZEN

As our girls are with rights of conquerors.

ADAM

Stop right there. Why are you running away;
Can't you see we bear the holy standard
Which unites us all, like brothers, in one cause?
We took our light of faith, the creed of love,
To Asia, that her savage hordes, where once
The holy cradle rocked to save us all,
Might feel its blessing. And would you now refuse
Your love to us?

FIRST CITIZEN

We've heard this speech before:
Our houses were soon blazing all the same.

They hurry away

ADAM
to the knights

Here you may see the cursed fruit of evil;
This is what happens when so many brigands
With base motives come waving the sacred flag
And slyly pander to the people's passions,
Proclaiming themselves their unappointed leaders.
My fellow knights! While our swords testify
To spotless virtue, to praise of God's great glory,
To womankind's defence and chivalry,
We are committed to restrain this monster—
To lead him counter to his own desires
That he may labour to more noble ends.

LUCIFER

Fine words, Tancred, but what happens when
The people begin to doubt your leadership...

ADAM

Where spirit lodges victory does too.
I'll crush them.—

LUCIFER

          And if they have their own spirit
Will you descend to meet it?

ADAM

          Why descend?
Is it not nobler to raise the creatures up?
To resign the field for lack of a few comrades
Is as contemptible as to refuse
The friendship of a man because one covets
His own share of the spoils.

LUCIFER

Alas, alas,
Your great ideals are all reduced to this.
It was for this, the bloodshed in the Circus,
For this franchisement of the individual?
A wondrous species of fraternity!

ADAM

Don't mock or think I fail to comprehend
The holy doctrines, the passion of my life.
Anyone who bears the sacred spark
And strives to join us—as he could and should—
Is heartily welcome, we will elevate him
To our ranks with one touch of the sword.
But we must guard the treasures of the order
Against the present all-engulfing chaos.
If only it would come, the day would come,
When barriers fall and all the world is pure,
Our redemption until then is incomplete.
But I would doubt the coming of that day
Had not the wheel been set in motion by
Our great and holy God Himself, in Person.
My friends, look round and see how you're received,
Alone in the great bustle of the city.
There's nothing for it, we must pitch our tents
In the nearest grove, as we have often done
Among the pagans. No doubt things will improve.
Begin the preparations. I will follow.
Each knight will answer for his soldiers' conduct.

The CRUSADERS *set up their camp*

LUCIFER

What a shame that all your fine ideas
Should bear only that old proverbial apple,
Sweet blushes outside, rotten inside.—

ADAM

                                      Stop!
Have you no faith in nobler things?

LUCIFER

And what use if I had when your kind lacks it?
This Order of Chivalry which you set up
For beacon in the midst of a wild sea
Will one day be snuffed out, and half-collapsed,
Prove more a hazard to brave travellers
Than simple rocks which never served for light.
Everything that lives, that sheds a blessing,
Must die sometime; the spirit leaves the body
Which remains behind like a corrupted corpse
Infecting the new world that grows around it
With its poisonous miasma. This is all
The great and glorious past bequeaths to us.

ADAM

It may be by the time our Order falls
Its sacred doctrines might have penetrated
The masses and diverted all the danger.

LUCIFER

The sacred doctrines! The very things that damn you
Each blessed time you stumble on them, since
You chop them so fine, sharpen them so neatly,
Refine them, twist them, that they drive you mad
Or turn to fetters. The human mind cannot
Sustain precise ideas—yet, in your pride,
It is precisely such that you are seeking—
And you destroy yourselves in search of it.
Examine this sword—a hair's breadth more or less
Will hardly change the nature of the weapon,

And so we could go on, reducing, adding:
At what precise point does the change occur?
Your senses will alert you in an instant
To alterations on a larger scale.
Why should I waste my breath to tell you this?
Just look around you. You need not look far.

A few CITIZENS *return*

ADAM

Dear friends, my men are tired and they need shelter
And surely here, within the capital
Of Christendom, they do not ask in vain.—

THIRD CITIZEN

The question is, are you a heretic?
That's worse than being a pagan.

FOURTH CITIZEN

                  Do you believe
In Homousion or Homoiusion?

ADAM

I don't understand.

LUCIFER

                  Refuse to tell them which.
It happens to be a burning issue here.

FOURTH CITIZEN

He hesitates. A heretic all right.

MORE CITIZENS

Have nothing to do with them. Let's lock our houses.
A curse on anyone who gives them shelter.

They depart. The PATRIARCH appears in full ceremonial dress, accompanied by his retinue from the palace. They are followed by a band of FRIARS escorting a chained group of HERETICS. Soldiers and citizens bring up the rear

ADAM

Astonishing. But who is that great prince
Approaching us, who looks so proud and arrogant?

LUCIFER

The Patriarch. The heir of the apostles.

ADAM

And that ugly bare-foot tribe of underlings
Who wear a false cloak of humility
And seem to take such pleasure in pursuing
The group in chains?

LUCIFER

      They're Christian cynics—friars.

ADAM

I've never seen their like among the hills
Back home.

LUCIFER

      Later you'll see more. You know
How slowly leprosy travels. Best be careful
Not to offend such absolutely virtuous
And therefore arrogant people.

ADAM

But what virtue
Could such a rabble possibly lay claim to?

LUCIFER

A virtue born of pain and self abasement,
As commanded by your Master on the Cross.

ADAM

But he employed them for the world's redemption—
These cowards here are committing blasphemy.
Like rebels they disdain the good Lord's grace.
It might be brave to shoot bears with a gun
But to take one to a gnat is idiotic.

LUCIFER

But if the gnat appears a bear to them
Are they not justified? And are they not
Right, in this heroic mood, to hound
Those who enjoy themselves—to hell if need be?

ADAM

I am like Thomas: I see but can't believe.
I shall confront these wonders face to face.

He approaches the PATRIARCH

We are Knights of the Holy Sepulchre, O Father,
Exhausted by our journey we need rest
But no one in the city will accept us.
You who have authority could help us.

PATRIARCH

My son, I fear I have no time to deal
With petty things. God's Glory and my flock
Require my services. I must pass judgment
On heretics like these who sow their poison
And spread like weeds. With fire and sword we prune them
But hell returns them to us every time
With greater strength. If you are truly soldiers
Of Christ why seek the distant Saracen?
Here you'll find more fearsome foes. Arise then,
Assault their strongholds, root them out, destroy
The old, the women, every girl and boy.

ADAM

Those harmless ones? You cannot wish that, Father.

PATRIARCH

The snake is harmless too while it is young
And then again once it has lost its fangs—
But would you spare it?

ADAM

                It must be a vile sin
Indeed to rouse such passionate anger in
The Church of Love.

PATRIARCH

                My son, love is not that
Which panders to the body, but that which guides
The spirit home, by fire or sword if need be,
To Him who said: I came not to bring peace
But war unto the world. These wicked infidels
Proclaim the idea of Homoiusion
In the mystic doctrine of the Trinity,
Although the True Church has declared the doctrine
Of Homousion an article of faith.

FRIARS

The fire is burning, to the stake with them!

ADAM

My friends, concede that single letter, 'i'
And you can make a nobler sacrifice
Crusading for the Holy Sepulchre.

AN OLD HERETIC

O lead us not into temptation, Satan.
We bleed, as God ordained, for the true faith.

FRIAR

Impertinence! To boast of the true faith.

OLD HERETIC

Is not the synod of Rimini with us,
And countless others?

FRIAR

              They were all misled.
Did not Nicea and other orthodox
Synods take our part?

OLD HERETIC

              Those apostates!
Impertinence indeed to try their strength
Against ours. What Fathers of the Church
Have you to match our Arius and both
Eusebiuses?

FRIAR

Could you produce a single
Athanasius?

OLD HERETIC

Where are your martyrs?

FRIARS

We have more than you!

OLD HERETIC

Oh yes, fine martyrs!
Lured to their deaths by visions of the devil.
I say to you, you are great Babylon,
That whore described by St John in his book,
Who'll perish in the full sight of the world.

FRIAR

The seven-headed Beast, the Antichrist!
St John knew all about you, what you are—
You curs and frauds, companions of the devil!

OLD HERETIC

You thieves, you snakes, you profligates, you gluttons...

PATRIARCH

Away with them, away. Don't waste your time.
Glory to God and to the stake with them.

OLD HERETIC

Glory to God! Well said, you foul corruption.
The sacrifice indeed is to God's glory.

You have the power and do as you desire,
But Heaven will judge whether your deeds are sound.
Already the hours of folly have been counted.
From our spilt blood fresh warriors will rise,
The idea survive, and that fierce flame which leaps
About us will shed light for centuries
To come. My friends, arise to death and glory!

HERETICS
singing in chorus

1. My God, my God, why hast thou forsaken me? why art thou
so far from helping me, and from the words of my roaring?
2. O my God, I cry in the daytime, but thou hearest not;
and in the night season, and am not silent.
3. But thou art holy... (Psalm 22)

FRIARS
interrupting with their own chorus

1. Plead my cause, O Lord, with them that strive with me:
fight against them that fight against me.
2. Take hold of shield and buckler, and stand up for mine help.
3. Draw out also the spear, and stop the way against them
that persecute me... (Psalm 35)

In the meantime the PATRIARCH *and the procession move on. A few*
FRIARS *carrying tracts mingle with the* CRUSADERS

LUCIFER

Why stand so silently? Why are you trembling?
You think this is a tragedy. Regard it
As comedy instead: it will amuse you.

ADAM

O do not joke about it! That one can die
So resolutely for the letter 'i'.
What then can we call sublime or noble?

116

LUCIFER

Whatever seems ridiculous to others.
The thickness of a hair divides the two—
Only some inner voice can judge between them,
And this close magistrate is sympathy
Which sanctifies or murders with its mockery.

ADAM

Why did I live to see such wickedness,
This skirmish in the proud domain of knowledge,
This deadly poison, masterfully extracted
From the freshest and most brilliant of flowers?
I knew it once when it was in full beauty,
At the testing time, when faith was persecuted.
What miscreant has wasted it and ruined it?

LUCIFER

It's victory herself that is to blame,
Breeding division, serving a hundred interests.
Defeat unites and propagates her martyrs
And gives such heretics their fortitude.

ADAM

I think I'd sooner throw away my sword
And go back to my homeland in the North
Where in the shadow of the ancient forests
A plain simplicity and manly honour
Might still defy this smooth age and its poison.
If only an inner voice did not keep whispering
That I would have to recreate that age.

LUCIFER

A vain endeavour. You can never set
The individual soul against the age.
Time is a stream that bears or covers you:

117

A man may swim in it but not direct it.
Those whom the historians call great
Are those who understood their century
And never entertained original thought.
Dawn does not come because the cocks are crowing:
The dawn comes first, then cocks begin to crow.
Those people there in chains, who hasten on
To martyrdom while insults rain on them,
See but one set of footprints leading onward;
It's from their ranks that new ideas arise;
They die for thoughts which their descendants breathe
Freely in with the common air. Enough.
Look at your camp—why are those scurvy friars
Tramping round it, trading, speechifying,
With weird outlandish gestures? Let us hear them.

FRIARS
surrounded by jostling CRUSADERS

Come buy, Crusaders, buy the saving doctrines
Of repentance, the answer to all questions.
It tells how long the murderer, the lecher,
The temple desecrator, and false witness
Are doomed to suffer in the fires of hell.
It also teaches how the rich may gain
A year's remittance through the payment of
Twenty solidi, while the poor pay three,
And those who lack the means may earn their pardon
By enduring a thousand lashes of the whip.
Who'll make a purchase of this splendid book?
Come buy!

CRUSADERS

One here.—And one here, holy father.

ADAM

The merchant's bad, the customers are worse.
Come, draw your swords and break up this foul market!

LUCIFER
in apparent confusion

I beg your pardon, this friar is an old friend.
And I have little quarrel with his kind,
As the Lord's stock has risen so has mine.
I fear you have not quite kept pace with us.

EVE *as* ISAURA *and* HELENA, *her maid, rush screaming to* ADAM *pursued by a few* CRUSADERS *who back off when they see him*

EVE
collapsing

Save me, conqueror!—

ADAM
assisting her

                    Peace now, noble lady,
You are safe here. Raise those lovely eyes.
How captivating!—Tell me what has happened.

HELENA

We had gone out in sheer delight of nature—
Seated in the deep shade of our garden,
Without a thought among the fragrant grasses
And hearing nothing but the nightingale,
When suddenly we saw two burning eyes
Maddened with lust, within a nearby thicket.
Frightened, we ran, pursued by four crusaders
Panting and pounding after us, who almost reached us,
And would have done so had we not found you.

ADAM

I don't know that I'd wish to wake you up.
What if you should leave me, like a dream?
How can the flesh be so transformed to spirit,
So noble and so fit for adoration?

LUCIFER

The flesh transformed to spirit! Could fate devise
A fitter punishment for foolish love
Than to realize the very qualities
Bestowed on the beloved by the lover?

ADAM

Some instinct tells me we have met before
And stood together at the throne of God.

LUCIFER

I beg you never to forget that love,
Which may be quite amusing as a duet,
Is inevitably tedious to third parties.

ADAM

She looks up—smiles. O bless you, merciful heavens.

EVE

You have saved me, Knight, how shall I thank you?

ADAM

Are not your words reward enough for me?

LUCIFER
to HELENA

Not even such a poor reward for me?

HELENA

What debt of gratitude do I owe you?

LUCIFER

Do you imagine that this noble knight
Intended to save you too? What vanity!
If a knight happens to rescue a fair lady
The squire is deemed to have saved the lady's maid.

HELENA

So what have I gained? Either I am grateful
And end up in the same spot as before,
Or ungrateful, and facing equal danger.
Those four crusaders weren't at all bad looking.

ADAM

O lady, command me. Where shall I escort you?

EVE

The convent doors are directly before us.

ADAM

The convent, you say? Surely its doors cannot
Debar me from my hope, O say they cannot!
Give me some favour to wear upon my cross
So that when I defend the faith in battle
I may remember this delightful vision
And never tire of waiting through long years
Until my race is won and the prize gained.

EVE

Take this ribbon.—

ADAM

Darker than night itself?
O lady, give me hope, give hope, not sorrow.

EVE

This is my favour—I can give no other.
Hope is not bred behind the doors of convents.

ADAM

Neither is love. And how could there not be love
Where you are, lady! What you are wearing shows
That you have not yet taken the veil.

EVE

Do not torment me further with your questions—
It hurts me so to see you suffering.

LUCIFER

Will you too be immured within those walls?

HELENA

Yes, but the key has not been thrown away.

LUCIFER

What a shame! I could have penned so sweet
An elegy for such a sad occasion.

HELENA

Get away with you, you sly deceiver!

LUCIFER

But why? Is it not grand to think of me
Scouring the sea-bed in search of your lost key?

HELENA

I would not trouble you so far.

LUCIFER

                  I'm going—
The monsters of the deep gape wide for me.

HELENA

Come back, come back, I fear for you so greatly—
Pick up the key at my windowsill instead.

ADAM

At least tell me your name, that in my prayers
I'll know for whom to plead, that I may call
Some blessing down on you, since you refuse
To let me share the sadness of your fate.

EVE

My name? Isaura. What is yours, sir knight?
A cloistered virgin is more used to prayer.

ADAM

Tancred is my name.

EVE

Farewell then, Tancred.

ADAM

Isaura, do not leave me quite so soon
Or you will make me curse the very name
I learned but now when you bade me farewell.—
A minute was too short for such a dream—
How can I continue to dream if you
Remain a mystery, if your fate yields
No golden thread to spin it out.

EVE

                              Then hear it.
My father, like you, was himself a knight
In the Order of the Holy Sepulchre.
One night they were surprised with fire and sword
And shouts of barbarians within the camp.
No hope remained of flight, and so he swore
To the Blessed Virgin that if he should escape
He'd offer me—a mere child then—to her.
He has returned and I, to keep his oath,
Have taken the sacrament.

ADAM

                    O blessed mother!
Embodiment of love at its most pure,
Did you not turn affronted from this scene
Of blasphemy, this stain upon your virtue,
Which turns the grace of Heaven to a curse?

HELENA
to LUCIFER

And don't you want to know my history?

LUCIFER

I know already: she loved, was cheated, then
Became deceiver when she loved again.
Once more she loved, but soon her lover bored her;
And now her vacant heart wants a new boarder.

HELENA

How uncanny! Are you friend to the devil?
I wouldn't have imagined you so modest
As to think my heart was short of a new guest.

LUCIFER
to ADAM

My lord, do hurry. You can't say farewell
And I cannot avoid making a conquest.

ADAM

Isaura, every word you speak is like
A sting in my heart. Sweeten the poison, lady,
With a kiss.

EVE

You heard my vow, knight, what can I do?

ADAM

But that cannot prevent me loving you!

EVE

Then you are happy, but how can I forget you?
O Tancred, I am weakening, I must go.
God be with you—we will meet in heaven.

ADAM

God go with you! I won't forget this day.

EVE *enters the convent*

HELENA
aside

And you, you coward—must I do everything?

aloud

The key is not in the ocean, you will find it
At my window.

She follows EVE

ADAM
recovering

We had better go.

LUCIFER

It's too late now, and there's an end to it.
You see the foolishness of all your kind
Who regard a woman merely as an object
Of passion, and brush the bloom of poetry
From her brow with horny hands, and rob yourself
Of love's most tender and enchanting blossom;
Then raise her, like a goddess, on an altar
And bleed for her and struggle pointlessly
While her kisses languish in sterility.—
Why not respect and honour her as a woman
Within the appointed sphere of womanhood?

In the meantime it has grown quite dark and the moon has risen. EVE *and*
HELENA *are seen at the window*

126

EVE

How longingly he looked at me and trembled,
This mighty hero trembled there before me,
But my maiden honour and my faith command me
And so I'm bound to suffer here like any
Sacrificial lamb.

HELENA

      The madness of our sex
Amazes me! For once we break the chains
Of prejudice we set off in pursuit
Of bestial pleasures, stripping off our masks
Of dignity, and roll about in mud
With wild abandon. If we leave the chains
Intact we go in fear of our own shadows
And allow our fairest charms to fade away,
Depriving us and others of their pleasure.—
Is there no middle way? I cannot see
What harm there can be in some brief encounter
Discreetly managed, a little love affair.
A woman, after all, is not a spirit.

EVE

Oh, Helena, look out, is he still waiting?
How could he have departed quite so lightly.
If only I could hear him speak again.

ADAM
to LUCIFER

Look back—is she not standing at the window,
Oh, will she not look out at me once more?
If only I could see her slender shape
Again—Isaura, forgive me waiting here.

EVE

Better for both of us for you to go.
A broken heart is quickly enough mended,
But broken again the pain is more intense.—

ADAM

Aren't you afraid when you look up at the night,
So silent and yet beating like a heart
For love that is forbidden us alone?
Aren't you afraid of falling under its spell?

EVE

All this exists in me like a faint dream
Come down from heaven to haunt me on the earth;
Waves of sweet music are flooding through the air,
I see a host of guardian angels smiling
Behind each bough with kisses on their lips.
But they no longer speak to us, dear Tancred.

ADAM

And why, oh why should this foul wall divide us?
So often have I breached the pagan ramparts,
Why should I not breach these walls just as well?—

LUCIFER

The spirit of the age defends these walls
And it is stronger than you, that is why.

ADAM

                                        Who says so?

A torch flares up in the background

20. Deliver my soul from the sword; my darling from the power of the dog.

21. Save me from the lion's mouth: for thou hast heard me from the horns of the unicorns.

22. I will declare thy name unto my brethren: in the midst of the congregation will I praise thee.   (Psalm 22)

EVE

O Lord have mercy on their sinful souls!—

ADAM
shrinking away

A dreadful hymn!

LUCIFER

It is your wedding march.

ADAM

So let it be, but I am not afraid.
For you, my love, I would dare anything.

CHORUS OF FRIARS
in the distance

26. ...let them be clothed with shame and dishonour that magnify themselves against me.

27. Let them shout for joy, and be glad, that favour my righteous cause: yea, let them say continually, Let the Lord be magnified, which hath pleasure in the prosperity of his servant.   (Psalm 35)

At the commencement of the above Psalm, ADAM, *who had advanced to the gate of the convent, stops again. An owl screeches from the tower, the air is filled with flying witches, and before the door a* SKELETON *rises from the ground and threatens* ADAM

EVE
slamming the window

God save us all!

SKELETON

Back from this hallowed porch!

ADAM

Who are you monster?

SKELETON

One who is sure to be
Present at all your kisses and embraces.

WITCHES
cackling

Sweet the sowing, sour the fruit,
Breed dove with serpent, we call out
Isaura!

ADAM

Ah, what dreadful shapes are these?
Have you transformed yourselves or is it I?
I knew you when you smiled and hoped to please.
What is dream here, what reality?
Your spell has bound my arms, I cannot move.—

LUCIFER

I have stumbled on congenial company.
I've waited long enough for luck like this,
Such seemly and attractive troupes of witches
Who far outbrazen any naked hussy,
And my terrifying old companion, death,
That twisted image of frigid virtue who
Will serve to repel the children of the earth.
All welcome! I regret I have no time
To while away the night with you in chatter.

The phantoms disappear

Arise, Tancred, arise! Your paramour
Has slammed the window; why should we stand here
All night? The wind blows cold, you'll catch a chill.
Helena's on her way, what should I do?
Should the devil go canoodling with a wench
He'd never live it down as long as he lived,
And he himself would dissipate his power.
It's strange how men with passion in their hearts
Will long and languish constantly for love
And reap mere pain. The devil's heart of ice
Escapes it only in the nick of time.

ADAM

Lead on, lead on to new life, Lucifer!
I took to arms for great ideals but found
Their application wicked and accursed,
Man sacrificed to satisfy God's honour,
And men sunk too low to achieve my goals.
I wanted to ennoble all our pleasures
But man has branded sweet delight with shame.
The sword of chivalry I held aloft
Has broken in my heart. To new terrain—
My value has been amply demonstrated,
I know now how to strive and to resign,
Can leave the field without disgrace. Let nothing

Henceforth set my soul on fire, the world
May go about its business as it pleases,
I shan't attempt to change its course again
But shall gaze with equanimity upon
Its foibles. I'm exhausted. I need rest.

LUCIFER

Rest then. But I hardly dare believe
That your spirit with its restless energy
Will let you rest for long. Follow me, Adam!

SCENE 8

In Prague. The garden of the Emperor's palace. An arbour to the right, an observatory tower to the left. Before it a spacious balcony with KEPLER's *writing desk, chair and astronomical instruments.* LUCIFER, *as* KEPLER's *apprentice, is seen on the balcony. In the garden* COURTIERS *and ladies are strolling about in groups, among them* EVE *as* BARBARA, *the wife of* KEPLER. *The* EMPEROR RUDOLF *is deep in conversation with* ADAM *as* KEPLER. *A heretic is being burned at the stake in the background. It is evening, turning into night. The* COURTIERS *pass before the scene.*

FIRST COURTIER

Another fellow getting nicely warm—
A witch or heretic this time?

SECOND COURTIER

             Who knows.
It's so unfashionable to enquire,
Only the riff-raff gather round the fire.
They don't even take much delight in it:
Nowadays they simply stare and mutter.

FIRST COURTIER

In my day we had festivals for such things—
The whole court, all of noble bloods were there.
Alas, the good old days don't last for ever.

They move on

LUCIFER

It's nice to have a fire on such chill nights,
I must admit that I've got used to it,
I fear, however, it must go out soon.
It won't be dowsed through manly resolution,

134

Nor through enlightened liberality,
But indifference in an age when no one's left
To throw logs on the fire. So I go cold.
All great ideals tend to meet their nemesis
Through petty errors in their premises.

He retires into the observatory. RUDOLF *and* ADAM *enter*

RUDOLF

Kepler, draw up my horoscope for me,
I had a bad dream last night and I fear
My star is in conjunction with some evil
Omen appearing in its radiance.
There, by the Snake's head. I've seen it before.

ADAM

All will be done, my lord, as you command.—

RUDOLF

When once the days of the climacteric
Are past we will commence on our new work
Which would have failed had we begun today.
I looked again through Hermes Trismegistus,
Synesius, Albertus, Paracelsus,
The Key of Solomon and other books
Before I found the error we had made.
When we contrived to make the Old King sweat
Then there appeared the Raven and the Lion,
And after them the Twofold Mercury
Emerged under their joint influence,
And the saline content of the precious stone,
The philosopher's, decreased and fell,
But we had overlooked Damp Fire, you see,
And Arid Water, and therefore failed to effect
The Sacred Knot, which should have crowned our efforts
With the elixir that rejuvenates old veins
And transmutes base metal into rarest gold.

135

ADAM

I understand, your highness.

RUDOLF

                    One word more.
I hear disturbing rumours in the court
That you have espoused new ideas, and take
A sieve to the doctrines of the Holy Church;
And further, while your mother is imprisoned
And facing the grave charge of sorcery,
You will certainly arouse suspicion by
Agitating so persistently
And publicly for her release.

ADAM

                    My lord,
She is my mother after all!

RUDOLF

                    My son,
The Holy Church is more truly your mother,
Forget the world: whatever is, is right;
Do not attempt to tinker with its works.—
Do I not shower all my gifts on you?
Your father, as you well know, kept an inn
And I raised you to high rank beyond dispute—
Though not without some difficulty, mind.
It's through your elevation to my throne
That you have gained the hand of Barbara Müller.
And that's why I repeat, take care my son.

He goes. ADAM *remains behind in deep thought, standing on the steps of
the balcony. Two* COURTIERS *pass before him*

THIRD COURTIER

The astrologer is deep in thought again.

FOURTH COURTIER

He is for ever careworn, the poor fellow.
He cannot acclimatise to this new sphere:
The peasant in him will keep slipping out.

THIRD COURTIER

He cannot understand that a true knight,
While worshipping a woman as a goddess,
Should always be prepared to shed his blood
If any scandal attaches to her name,—
He is morbidly suspicious of flirtation.

EVE, *with another group, joins the two* COURTIERS *and laughing taps the*
SECOND COURTIER *on the shoulder with her fan*

EVE

Off with you, sir—for God's sake pity me
Or I shall die with laughing at your jokes.
But look, here are two po-faced gentlemen.
Have you two men by any chance imbibed
That damnable new innovative spirit?
Oh out of my sight! I really cannot stand
Their spleen and envy and their gloomy notions.
Reproachful of this world of brilliant calm
And contemplating other ways of life.

THIRD COURTIER

We plead Not Guilty to the charge, dear lady.
Who'd wish for change when graced by your good presence.

First Courtier

But if I'm not mistaken there I see
A man with signs of worry on his face.

Eve

My poor husband? Gentlemen, for God's sake
And to please me, do eliminate him
From your list of suspects, seeing we are bound
By sacred ties—and he is ill, quite ill.

Second Courtier

An invalid, perhaps, to your bright eyes?

Third Courtier

Indeed! And does he dare—as no one would—
Insult you with his envy and suspicion?
If only I could be your knight, I'd fling
My gauntlet in the wretched fellow's face.

In the meantime they have come up to Adam

My dear professor, I'm so pleased to see you,
I want to take a trip to my estates
And need a weather forecast.

First Courtier

                    As for me
I'd like a horoscope drawn for my son,
Born yesterday, a little after midnight.

Adam

Both will be done by morning, gentlemen.

Fourth Courtier

The party is breaking up, we too should go.

THIRD COURTIER

Your staircase, madam—I must bid you good night.

Whispering

An hour from now.

EVE
whispering

The far side of the arbour.

Aloud

Good night, gentlemen.—Come along, dear Johann!

They all depart. ADAM and EVE are left on the balcony. ADAM sinks into an armchair. EVE stands before him. It is rapidly darkening

EVE

Johann, my dear, I'm rather short of money.

ADAM

I haven't a farthing, you've had everything.

EVE

And must I therefore suffer this eternal
Penury? The ladies of the court
Go strutting like peacocks, and I am ashamed
To be seen among them. Why, whenever some lord
Bows to me and tells me, full of smiles,
That I'm the queen of the whole company,
I blush for you, that you permit your queen
To attend the court in such a shabby outfit.

ADAM

Do I not wear myself out, night and day?
I prostitute my knowledge for your sake,
Polluting it with useless weather forecasts
And drawing up of useless horoscopes.
I hide the truth I recognize at heart
And propagate what I know to be false.
And if I blush for shame it is because
I'm lower than the Sibyls who at least
Believe in their own forecasts while I don't.
I do it all for you, to win your favour.
What should I do with the wages of my sin
Since I require nothing in this world
Except the night and all its glimmering stars,
Only the hidden harmony of the spheres?
The rest is yours. And bear in mind that when
The Emperor's coffers are empty now and then
My wages must wait however I may nag.
What hurts me most is that although I give you
All my morning's pay, you're never grateful.

EVE
weeping

You dare reproach me with your sacrifices!
Have I not sacrificed enough for you?
When I, the daughter of a noble family,
Staked my whole future on your dubious rank,
And was it not through me you were accepted
In polite society? Deny it, wretch.—

ADAM

Are science and spirit then of dubious rank?
That beam of heavenly light upon my brow,
Is that indeed of shady pedigree?
What nobility can stand beside it?
That which you call noble is mere dust,

A crumbling idol whence the soul has fled,
But mine is ever young and powerful.—
If only you could understand me, woman,
If only your soul and mine were kindred spirits
As once I thought they were when we first kissed,
You would be proud of me and would not seek
Your happiness outside my sphere of being;
You would not parade all that is sweet in you
Before the world, and save all that is bitter
For home and hearth.—Oh woman, how I loved you!
And love you still, but O how bitter is
The sting that sours the honey of my heart.
It hurts me to think how high your soul could be
If you were truly free to be a woman;
That fate which makes an idol of a woman,
Who was a goddess in the great good days
Of chivalry, when they believed in such things,
Has crushed you. No one in this age of dwarfs
Believes: this mummery is just a cloak
For vice. I'd tear my heart out and divorce you,
However it hurt, if I could find some peace,
And you too might be happier without me;
But there again we come up against custom:
Authority, commandments of the Church,
So we must bear each other till we die.

He hides his head in his hands. EVE *is moved and strokes him*

EVE

My dear Johann, don't take it so to heart
If now and then I say things out of turn,
I don't want you to fall into despair.
But look, the Court is such a splendid place,
The ladies are so haughty and sarcastic,
How could I begin to argue with them?
You're not so angry with me anymore?
Good night. Remember—money in the morning.

She goes down the stairs and into the arbour

ADAM

What a miraculous mixture of high and low
Is woman, a blend of nectar and pure poison.
Then why does she attract us? Because she is
Good in herself: the age that gave her birth
Has made her evil. Hey, apprentice!

LUCIFER *comes with a lamp and puts it down on the table*

LUCIFER

Master?

ADAM

A weather forecast and a horoscope
Are needed. Prepare the things immediately.

LUCIFER

Something brilliant and glittering, no doubt:
Who'd pay good money for unvarnished truth?

ADAM

Don't go too far—nothing ridiculous.

LUCIFER

It's well nigh impossible to invent
A prophecy to scandalise the parents.
Is not each new born child the new Messiah,
The family's own Star of Betlehem?
It's only later that it grows into
A common brat.

He writes. In the meantime EVE *has reached the arbour.*
The THIRD COURTIER *goes to meet her*

THIRD COURTIER

You cruel hearted creature,
How long you've kept me suffering out here.

EVE

It seems such a great sacrifice for you
To put up with a chill breeze of an evening
While I betray a good and noble husband!
For you, sir, I defy the curse of heaven
And attract the censure of society.

THIRD COURTIER

Neither the curse of heaven, nor society's
Censure can pierce the darkness of this grove.

ADAM
musing

I longed for an age which had no need of struggle,
Where no one upset the settled scheme of things
Or interfered with all its hallowed customs,
Where I could rest and smile indifferently
And heal the wounds of my incessant battles.—
That age is here, but what use if the heart
Contains a soul—that sacred, painful heirloom
Obtained from heaven by man who is a fool—
Which longs to act and will not let him rest,
Which leaps to combat with his sluggish pleasures.—
Apprentice, ho! Bring wine, I'm shivering,
I'll have to set this arctic world ablaze.
An age of midgets calls for some Dutch courage
To wash away the dirt which clings to us.—

LUCIFER *brings wine.* ADAM *continues sipping it throughout what follows*

Oh infinite heavens, open, open up
Your hidden sacred volumes to my sight!

If only I could learn your laws I might
Forget the age and everything around me.
You are eternal, everything else passes,
You raise me up while all else drags us down.

THIRD COURTIER

Oh, Barbara, if only you were mine!
If only God would take away your husband
So that he might see heaven all the clearer,
Since that is what he spends his life observing.

EVE

Hush sir, or I'll pity the poor creature
So dreadfully my tears might stop my kisses.

THIRD COURTIER

You're joking with me.

EVE

Not at all, it's true.

THIRD COURTIER

Who understands these mysterious moods of yours?
This shows you cannot love me, Barbara.
If I were exiled or impoverished
Tell me what you'd do to help your lover?—

EVE

In all sincerity I could not tell you.

ADAM

Oh for a time to melt this frozen order,
To confront its worn out lumber with new vigour,
To rise like a judge, to punish or reward

He rises and totters to the edge of the balcony

Not to shrink from drastic measures or from
Pronouncing the mystic word, which like an avalanche
Would thunder down its destined course and crush
The very man perhaps who uttered it.

The strains of the Marseillaise are heard

I hear it now, the anthem of the future,
I've found the word, that mighty talisman
To revive the ancient world in all its freshness.

SCENE 9

The scene suddenly changes to the marketplace of the Place de la Grève in Paris. The balcony becomes a scaffold, the table a guillotine, beside which stands LUCIFER *in the role of* EXECUTIONER. ADAM *as* DANTON, *addresses a milling crowd from the side of the scaffold. A company of ragged* RECRUITS *appears to the sound of drums. They form a line around the scaffold. Bright sunlight.*

ADAM
as if continuing his speech from the previous scene

Liberty, Equality, Fraternity!—

CROWD

And death to those who fail to recognize them!

ADAM

I quite agree. Two battlecries preserve
Our great ideal from universal menace,
One we address to those good souls we trust:
'France is in danger', and that wakes them up.
The other we must thunder out to traitors:
It is but one word, 'Tremble'—and they perish.
These rose up kings against us and we threw
A head to them—a head of state—the king's;
The priests rose up against us, and we wrested
The lightning from their hands and reinstated
Reason, that ancient exile, on the throne.
But neither does our other call grow fainter,
And our best men still heed the country's summons.
We have eleven armies at the front
And a constant stream of brave young men step forth
To fill the gaps left by our fallen heroes.
Who says that madness and the lust for blood
Must decimate our country in due course?

You smelt the ore, the dross is drained away,
The better part remains, is purified.
And what if here and now we call for blood—
Let them think us monsters, I don't mind,
My name may be accursed for all I care,
Providing France be powerful and free.

RECRUITS

We only ask for arms and one to lead us!

ADAM

That's right, that's right! You only call for arms
Despite the fact that you lack all things else:
Your clothes are ragged and your feet are naked,
With bayonets though you'll make up your losses
Because you'll win. The people can't be conquered.
One general has just been executed
For leading our brave soldiers to defeat.

THE CROWD

The traitor!

ADAM

　　　　Yes, you're right. The people have
No treasure but their blood which they shed nobly
And prodigally for their country's sake.—
Whoever has the nation's sacred treasure
At his command and fails to conquer all
Is deemed a traitor.—

An OFFICER *steps out from the ranks of the* RECRUITS

OFFICER

> Put me in his place
Then, citizen. I'll wipe out his disgrace.

ADAM

Your confidence is honourable, friend—
Before we place such trust in you, however,
You must deserve it on the field of battle.

OFFICER

That trust lives in my soul. As for the rest—
I too possess a head which may be worth
As much or more than that which has just fallen.

ADAM

Who'll guarantee you'll bring it if I ask you?

OFFICER

What better guarantor could you desire
Than I myself who hold my life as nothing?

ADAM

That's not the way that most young people talk.

OFFICER

But citizen, I ask you just once more—

ADAM

Have patience, you have time to reach your goal.

OFFICER

I see you do not trust me. You must learn
To think better of me citizen.—

He shoots himself in the head

ADAM

                                        A pity—
He deserved the opposition's bullet.
Take him away, my friends.—We'll meet again
Once victory is ours.

The RECRUITS *march away*

Oh how I wish
That I could share your fate. But my lot is to struggle
Without glory—my death in action yields
No honour but a foe who plots and watches
And lies in wait for me and hallowed France.

CROWD

Point him out to us and he shall die!

ADAM

The one I could point out is dead already.

CROWD

What about the suspects then? Whoever
Falls under suspicion is already
Guilty, he is branded: the instinct of
The people is infallible, a prophet.—
Death to the aristocracy. On, on,
Into the prisons, we shall be the judges,
The judgment of the populace is sacred.

The CROWD *moves off towards the prison*

ADAM

There is no danger there, the bars are strong,
The fetid air that kills both mind and body
Is on your side already. Let them be.
Real bare-faced treason laughs and whets its blade
On benches at the heart of the Convention.

CROWD

To the Convention then—it still needs purging!—
The Convention can come later, we can practise
On the prisons in the meantime. While we do,
Prepare a list of all the traitors, Danton.

The CROWD *moves off threateningly. A few* SANS-CULOTTES *have dragged a young* MARQUIS *and his sister,* EVE, *before the scaffold*

SANS-CULOTTE

Another pair of young aristocrats:
Their proud faces and this fine white linen
Are clear proofs of their guilt!

ADAM

                              A noble couple.
Step up here, young people.

SANS-CULOTTE

                              We'll be off now
To join our comrades. There's a job to do,
And traitors to be punished.

The SANS-CULOTTES *go with the others. The young couple step on to the scaffold. Only a few guards remain behind*

151

Adam

I do not understand what draws me to you
But I will risk my life to save you both.

Marquis

Danton, no. If we indeed are guilty
And you excuse us, then you are a traitor:
If we are not we don't require your mercy.

Adam

Who are you to talk like this to Danton?

Marquis

I am a marquis.

Adam

        Wait—are you aware
Our one form of address is Citizen?

Marquis

I'm not aware His Majesty the King
Has abolished titles.

Adam

        Hold your tongue, you fool.
The very guillotine is listening.—
But join us and a new career awaits you.

Marquis

I have no royal permit, citizen,
To join a foreign army.

ADAM

Then you'll die.

MARQUIS

Then I will swell the ranks of my relations
Who gave their lives defending the King's cause.

ADAM

Why must you rush so blindly to your death?

MARQUIS

Do you believe this noble privilege
Is preserved only for members of your class?—

ADAM

So you defy me? Good, I'll take you on.
Who'll win? I'll rescue you against your will.
A future and more tranquil generation
In whom the spirit of faction has turned to ashes
Will praise me for this. National Guard! Come,
Take him to my house, look after him.

The MARQUIS *is escorted away by a few members of the National Guard*

EVE

Be strong, my brother!

MARQUIS

And God protect you, sister!

He goes

EVE

Here is a head, no worse than Roland's was.

ADAM

Let not such hard words pass your tender lips.

EVE

More tender words do not become a scaffold.

ADAM

This dread contraption is my daily business.
When you appeared on it a piece of heaven
Alighted there and locked me in its sanctum.

EVE

Even the priests refrain from mockery
When sacrificial beasts are herded past them.

ADAM

It is I who am the sacrifice, believe me.
Though other men may envy me my power,
Joyless and despising life and death,
I see my throne beside which, day by day,
Men lose their heads, and I await my turn—
Knee deep in blood, my solitude torments me;
I long for the relief of loving someone.
If only for a day you could instruct me
In this heavenly science, woman, I would calmly
Lay my head on the block the morning after.

EVE

In a world of terror you still look for love—
Have you no conscience left to terrify you?

ADAM

To possess a conscience is the privilege
Of common people; those who are led by fate
Have little enough time for introspection.
Have you ever known a storm to hesitate
Because some tender rose fell in its path?
Then who would be so foolish as to pass
Judgment on the leaders of the people?
Who can see the wires that move a Brutus
Or Catiline across the public stage?
There might be some who think that famous men
Have altogether quit the human race
And exist in some superior mode of being
Untouched by petty trials and tribulations,
And unaffected by routine affairs.—
Don't you believe them—the heart continues beating
On the throne: If Caesar had a lover
She might have thought him merely a nice boy
And it probably would not have crossed her mind
That the whole world lay trembling at his feet.
This being so, please tell me, tell me why
You could not love me? Are we not man and woman?
They say whatever loves and hates we bear
Within our hearts we have inherited:
I feel my heart is somehow bound to yours,
Is this so difficult to understand?

EVE

And if I did, what then? You're led by one god,
My heart is given to another.
How could we ever understand each other!

ADAM

Abandon your outmoded concepts then,
Why sacrifice yourself to exiled gods?
Besides, there is but one befitting altar
For a woman: one ever young—the heart.

EVE

Neglected altars may still claim their martyrs.
Oh Danton, it is nobler to preserve
And tend a ruin lovingly than hail
A rising power; this is the vocation
Most appropriate to woman's nature.

ADAM

No man has ever seen me moved to tears,
And could they see me now, good friend or foe,
They'd marvel that a man whom fate has driven
To purge the world like an engulfing storm
Should tarry on the scaffold, the tears burning
In his eyes for love of a young girl:
Oh how they'd laugh and prophesy the fall
Of Danton, and not one of them would fear him.
Grant me one ray of hope, I beg of you.

EVE

When once beyond the grave your soul finds peace,
Shakes off the bloody dust of our own age
Then perhaps…

ADAM

                Don't, don't go on, dear girl,
I've no belief in such an afterlife,
I struggle on with fate in no such hope.—

The CROWD *returns in a fierce mood, their weapons bloody, heads are
stuck on lances. A few of them push their way onto the scaffold*

CROWD

Justice is done—they were a haughty lot.

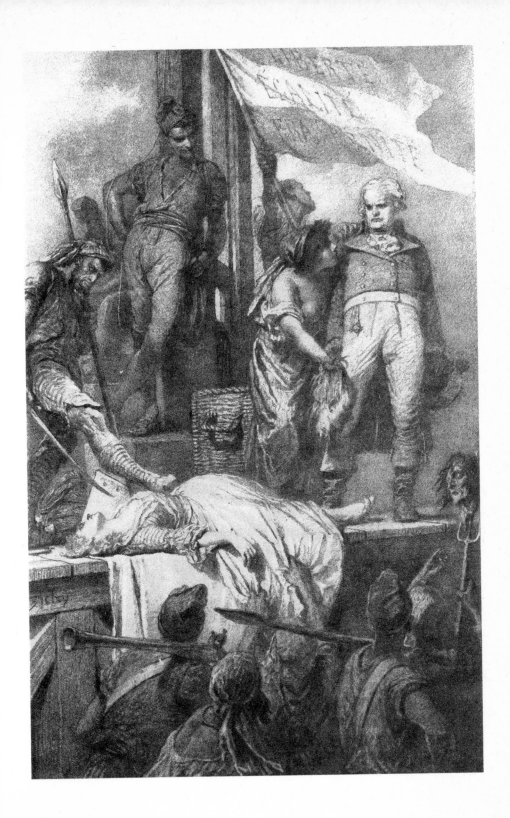

A Sans-Culotte
handing Danton *a ring*

Here is a ring to swell the country's coffers.
One of those wastrels pressed it in my hand
As I was about to cut his throat. His type
Believe that we are robbers, pure and simple.—
What, you're still alive?—Go join your fellows.

He stabs Eve *who falls at the back of the scaffold*

Adam
covering his eyes

And now she's dead.—Ah fate, who can resist you?

Crowd

Now on to the Convention. Lead us, citizen.—
Have you prepared the list of traitors' names?

The Crowd *moves away from the scaffold.* Eve *as a ragged and excited*
Working Girl *detaches herself from them and rushes to* Danton,
a dagger in one hand, a bloody head in the other

Eve

Danton, look at this conspirator—
He would have killed you but I killed him first.

Adam

If he could have performed my duties better
You did badly—if not, you've done well.

Eve

Oh I've done well, and I want my reward:
I want to spend a night with you, great man.

158

ADAM

What sympathy has sprung up in your breast?
What tender feelings can a tigress harbour?

EVE

Really, citizen, it seems you've joined
Those blue-blooded aristocrats or grown
Delirious and babble of romance.
You are a man, and I am a young woman.
My admiration draws me to you, great one.

ADAM
aside

She sends cold shivers down me—I can't look,
I cannot bear this dreadful phantasm.
What a miraculous likeness!—Only those
Who have seen angels and looked back to find
The angel fallen can have seen the like.
Her features, figure, voice, and everything
Identical, the difference is so small
That what she lacks could not be written down,
And yet the whole effect is alien!—
One's sanctity protected her from me,
But this repels me with the stench of hell.—

EVE

What are you muttering to yourself?

ADAM

                        I'm counting
Madam, and find that I have fewer nights
Remaining than are traitors in the country.

CROWD

On to the Convention—name the culprits!

In the meantime ROBESPIERRE, SAINT-JUST *and other members of the Convention arrive with a fresh crowd and set up a new platform*

SAINT-JUST

How could he name them? He is the arch traitor.—

The CROWD *grows agitated*

ADAM

You dare accuse me, Saint-Just! Don't you know
How powerful I am?

SAINT-JUST

           You were. The people
Made you so, but they are wise—they know
And sanctify the word of the Convention.

ADAM

I recognize no higher authority
Than the people—the people are my friends.

More agitation in the CROWD

SAINT-JUST

Your friends are the opponents of the country.
The noble people will pass judgment on you.
Before them all I charge you, Danton, traitor:
With embezzlement of state funds, sympathy
With aristocracy, and lust for power
Of the most tyrannical, despotic kind.

ADAM

Take care, Saint-Just, my words will strike you down.
Your charges are all false!

ROBESPIERRE

                    Don't let him speak—
You know his tongue is cunning as a serpent's.
Arrest him in the name of Liberty.

CROWD

Ignore him, let's not listen, let him perish!

They surround him and take hold of him

ADAM

Don't listen then, but neither shall I hear
Your accusations. We shan't convince each other
With speeches, neither shall your actions sway me.
You have simply anticipated me,
O Robespierre, no more, don't boast of it.
I myself lay down my arms—enough.—
I take this occasion though to summon you
To follow me before three months are out.
Look sharp, headsman, for you dispatch a giant.

He lays his head on the block

SCENE 10

Everything suddenly changes back to as it was in Scene 8. ADAM *is* KEPLER *once more, his head resting on his desk.* LUCIFER, *his* APPRENTICE, *stands beside him and taps him on the shoulder. The morning is dawning grey.*

LUCIFER

The execution is postponed for now.—

ADAM
rising

Where am I, and where are all my dreams?

LUCIFER

They've flown with your intoxication, sir.

ADAM

Are times so low that only drunkenness
Can rouse my aging breast to dreams of greatness?
What splendid visions rose before my eyes!
One must be blind to miss that heavenly spark
However it's defaced with blood and grime,
The good and evil on such vast proportions
That both of them appeared miraculous.
It was the stamp of power that amazed me.
Why did I wake? So I should see this age
Of dwarfishness confirmed, this age which masks
Corruption with its smiles and lying manners.

LUCIFER

You're feeling flat—I know the state of mind,
It's just the morning of the night before.

EVE
stepping from the arbour

Be off with you—I see that my suspicions
Were well founded. You dare suggest to me
That I should kill my husband! You think that I,
Your so-called idol, should descend so low?

COURTIER

For heaven's sake, collect yourself, my love;
Think of the scandal if we should be heard.

ADAM

Were those two women also just a dream?
What am I saying? One woman, two forms,
Who changed abruptly as my fortune changed,
Like waves that pulse between the light and dark.

EVE

I see—for you the scandal is what matters!
The crime is less important if it's hidden,
You irreproachable figure of a knight!
Oh fie on you, you mock a helpless woman
Till she casts aside the well-established virtues
Of maidenhood and prejudice, and then
You sneer and condescend, regarding her
A lowly instrument of your own vices.
I never want to see you again, now go!

COURTIER

This is too much. To make a song and dance
Of such a trivial matter is enough
To turn us into a common laughing stock.
We'll meet again and smile, and even flirt
And never mention what has passed between us.
Good morning, madam!

He goes

EVE

        Miserable wretch!—
But here I am with all my sins and tears.

She goes

ADAM

A dream, that's all it was, and now it's over.
But not quite everything. Ideas are stronger
Than fallen matter. One can be destroyed
By violence, the other is eternal.
And I can see my own ideas growing
Progressively purer, gaining nobility,
However slowly, till they fill the world.

LUCIFER

The sun is rising. Time for your lecture, sir.
Your youthful audience has arrived, impatient
To glean your words of scientific wisdom.

He rings the bell attached to the tower of the observatory

ADAM

Don't mock me with this talk about my science,
It makes me blush to hear men praise me for it.

LUCIFER

But don't you teach a lot of clever students?

ADAM

I don't teach them, I only keep them busy
With words which they don't understand. They have
No sense of what to do or not to do.
Ignorant people tend to gawp and think

164

We conjure up some spirit with fine words,
The whole thing is a trick and nothing more
To hide the clever work of charlatans.

A PUPIL *hurries towards them and steps on to the balcony*

PUPIL

It was generous of you to call me, sir,
Promising to quench my thirst for knowledge,
To let me peer into the heart of things
More deeply than you see fit to let others.

ADAM

Indeed, your industry is so outstanding
The privilege is amply justified.

PUPIL

So here I am, heart shaking with desire
To pry into the laboratory of nature.
To grasp it all and to enjoy it better,
To feel that I'm securely in command
Of both material and spiritual realms.

ADAM

You want too much. A mere speck in the world,
How could you see the splendour of the whole?—
You want dominion, knowledge, satisfaction—
You'd have to be a god to bear the weight
Of all this on your back and not collapse.
If you desired less you might attain it.

PUPIL

Whichever mystery you choose to solve,
Great scientist, I'm sure to gain by it,
Since I so keenly feel my ignorance.

Adam

Very well then, I see that you are worthy,
And I will lead you to the utmost altar
To see the truth as I myself conceive it.
We can't be overheard by common students?
The truth is terrible and could be lethal
If the people were to hear about it now.
There'll come a time—would it were here already—
When all this will be spoken in the streets,
But not until the people come of age.—
Now give me your hand, and swear not to betray
What you're about to learn.—So, listen then.—

Pupil

I'm all a-tremble with desire and fear.

Adam

Just what was it you said before, my boy?

Pupil

I said I did not understand a thing.

Adam
carefully

Neither do I, nor anyone else, believe me.
Philosophy is just the poetry
Of those things that we can't yet comprehend.—
It is the most amenable of studies
Since, in a nightmare world, it is content
To amuse itself in the most docile fashion.
It has countless other kindred disciplines
Which frown and draw their figures in the sand,
Which call a line a vortex, or proclaim
The circle a sacred shape. The gravity

And eloquence of it is farcical:
Enough to make you laugh once you see through it.
For all the time men go in fear and trembling,
Edging round those diagrams in the sand,
Dreadful snares await the foolhardy
Who overstep the mark and lose their way.
And there stands folly, ever vigilant,
Obstructive in the name of piety,
The guardian of whatever powers may be.

PUPIL

I see, I see. And will it always be so?

ADAM

No, one day they will laugh at all of this.
The statesmen whom we now consider great,
The orthodox at whom we gawp in wonder,
Will then appear as mere comedians,
And genuine greatness will assume their place:
The simple man, the man of nature, he
Who only leaps when he perceives a ditch
Or takes a road once he can see it clear.
And science, which now often leads to madness
By virtue of its tangled threads, will then
Be understood by all though learned by none.

PUPIL

This then is that clear and simple language
The apostles must have spoken.—But even if
The rest is nothing but mere useless lumber,
Don't rob me of my faith in art, to know which
One must understand the principles.

ADAM

Even in art the true perfection lies
In concealing art from the observer's eyes.

PUPIL

Should we content ourselves then with hard fact?
Idealization gives our work its soul.

ADAM

You're right: idealization gives it soul
And raises it to parity with nature
And validates its true creative life
Without which it would be dead artifice.
But do not think that by idealizing
You can outstrip the living force of Nature.
And as for rules and patterns, let them be.
If man is strong and God resides in him
He'll be an orator, or carve, or sing,
He'll weep with all his heart when he is low
And smile in his sleep after a bout of pleasure.
And if he breaks new ground he'll reach his goal.—
New rules will spring directly from his art:
Abstraction forges principles, not wings,
Though it might well serve to fetter dwarfish souls.

PUPIL

What should I do then, master? Please advise me.
Have I sacrificed so many nights to science
To attain only this parity with fools?
Have I wasted all my time without reward?

ADAM

No, for this alone gives you the right
To reject all its temptations and advances.
One who has never looked danger in the face
Is a coward if he retreats. But seasoned soldiers
May ignore a brawler yet remain courageous,
No shadow of suspicion attends courage.—
So take these yellow folios and parchments
And throw the mildewed things onto the fire.

169

They stop us standing on our own two feet,
Prevent us thinking for ourselves, transmit
The accumulated errors of the past
Like prejudices to the coming world.
To the fire with them! Now, out into fresh air.
Why should you learn the meaning of a song
Or the nature of a forest while your life
Diminishes behind these joyless walls
Of dust. You think your life is long enough
To spend your dying days in theory?
Together we will take leave of the school.
Your golden youth should lead you to the joys
Of songs and sunlight; as for me, lead on
My cynical guardian spirit, to the world
That is to be, providing it can grasp
Great men's ideals, and let our hidden thoughts
Speak freely above the cursed dust of ruins.

SCENE 11

London. A marketplace between The Tower and The Thames. The bustle of
a noisy and colourful crowd. ADAM, *as a man of mature years, stands with*
LUCIFER *on one of the bastions of The Tower. Twilight.*

CHOIR
mingling with the noise of the crowd, accompanied by soft music

Life's an ocean, roaring, tidal,
Every breaker bears a world,
One flung upward, one dragged downward,
Who cares which way they are hurled?—
You fear now for the individual
Engulfed by masses, then you feel
For millions of vanquished subjects
Ground under the tyrant's heel.
You fear for Poetry the one day,
The state of Science ruins the next,
Lock the waves up in your system,
Bind the breakers in a text.
Struggle as you will, grow weary,
Water's all you stand to gain,
The roaring splendour of the ocean
Laughs and thunders in disdain.
Let it thunder, life will govern
All the strands of her domain.
Nothing's lost, however many
Battles she may fight. The years
Pass and leave her ever youthful:
Her siren voice attends your ears.

ADAM

This is the world I always hungered for,
My path lay through a maze until this vision,
But now the way lies clear in front of me,
I hear the cheerful song of competition.

LUCIFER

Like hymns it sounds good from a certain height,
All croaks and sighs and moans are sweetly mingled
And sound delightful once they reach us here.—
God hears it this way too, and that is why
He thinks his world is such a great success.
Down there, however, it sounds rather different,
There you can hear the beating of its heart.

ADAM

You sceptical old mocker, isn't this
A finer world than those you've dragged me through?
The overgrown retaining walls have crumbled,
The terrifying ghosts once showered with honours,
That they might torment the future, have all gone.
Free competition opens up the road,
No pyramids, nor slaves to bear the load.

LUCIFER

From such a height you'd not have heard the sound
Of slaves groaning in Egypt, come to that;
In other ways the work is quite sublime!
From such a height, do not the noble people
Of Athens appear to act most prudently
In sacrificing one great, kindly man
In order to forestall some likely danger;
And do we not, for similar reasons, shun
Effeminate tears and such prevarications?

ADAM

Now that's enough, you obstinate old sophist!

LUCIFER

Assume you're right—the groans have died away.
What we have now is a vast level plain.—

172

What peaks attract us? Or what depths? What fears?
Where is life's variety and sweetness?
No shining floods, no tussling with the sea—
It's all mud flats, a colony of toads.

ADAM

We have the common good for compensation.

LUCIFER

Look, from this high perch we may pass judgment
On life as it crawls by beneath our feet
Just as the historical writers do.
They hear no groaning or cracked voices. All
They hear is the faint music of the past.

ADAM

I see that even Satan grows romantic
Or else doctrinaire. That's quite a landmark.

LUCIFER
pointing to The Tower

No wonder, since the very spot we stand on
In the modern world is haunted by the past.

ADAM

I've no use for this broken down old tower,
I'm happy to descend to the new world,
I do not doubt that I will rediscover
Ideals and poetry within its waves.—
It may well be that they no longer rend
The sky in open and titanic struggle,
But in their modest way they may create
A world that is more human, more attractive.

LUCIFER

It would indeed be pointless to doubt that.
As long as the material world exists
My power to negate its opposite
Remains. While men have hearts and minds that can
Conceive ideas, and while authority
Persists in circumscribing their desires,
Ideas and poetry, in their own way,
Their proper spheres, will go saying No.—
But what shape do you think we ought to take
Before we join that busy crowd below?
The way we're dressed we cannot leave this mound,
Where images of ancient days swirl round.

ADAM

What shapes you like. Thank heaven, no man stands
Above his fellows now. And so to know
Their hearts let's mingle with the throng below!

They both descend into The Tower, and emerge below, dressed as labourers.
They mingle with the crowd. A PUPPETEER *is standing by his booth, on which*
there squats a little scarlet coated monkey on a chain

PUPPETEER

This way, this way, my fine gentlemen,
The performance will begin in half a minute.
The piece is a delightful comedy
In which you'll see the Serpent as he tempts
Our mother Eve, whose curiosity
Succeeds in bringing down her husband Adam.
And you will see this agile little monkey
Impersonate man with great dignity;
And after that a bear plays dancing master.
Step this way, my fine gentlemen, this way!

The crowd jostle around his booth

LUCIFER

Hear that, Adam? They're talking about us.
It must be nice to have been given a part
That even after twice three thousand years
Still has the youngsters rolling in the aisles.

ADAM

A joke in poor taste. Come on, let's be going.

LUCIFER

Poor taste? Just look how they're enjoying it,
Those red-cheeked lads who half an hour ago
Were dozing at their desks with dull old Nepos.
And who is to say who's right? The ones who stride
Through life, conscious of their waking power,
Or those with tired brains who stumble out?—
Do you derive more pleasure from your Shakespeare
Than they do from this monstrous taradiddle?

ADAM

The monstrosity of it is what disturbs me.

LUCIFER

The air of Greece still clings to you. Now listen,
I am the son—or father, if you will,
It makes no difference in the spirit world—
Of a new movement called Romanticism
And I take special joy in monstrous sights.
An apelike grin across the human face;
No purity—a mud pie in its place;
All feelings twisted, hair-shirts for remorse,
And pious hymns out of the mouths of whores;
The flattery of mean things, pettiness;
The burned-out rakehell cursing tenderness—
These help me to forget my lost domain:
I change my shape, and lo! I live again.

PUPPETEER
tapping ADAM's *shoulder*

How come you're in the front row of the stalls,
Bird-brain? Only those who are tired of life
And ready to hang themselves, give shows for free.

ADAM *and* LUCIFER *move off. A young* FLOWER GIRL *appears, selling*
violets

FLOWER GIRL

Sweet violets, the first blooms of the year,
The messengers of spring. Come buy from me!
This tender flower provides the orphan's bread
And lends the poor a touch of finery.—

A MOTHER
buying some violets

I'll take a few to deck my poor dead child.

ANOTHER GIRL
also buying

They're sure to look nice with my long dark hair.

FLOWER GIRL

Sweet violets, come gentlemen, come buy!

She moves away

A JEWELLER
in his booth

Those weeds are always our competitors
And we can never drive them out of fashion.

A lovely neck should only be adorned
With precious pearls—for after all, that's why
The diver braves the perils of the deep,
Confronting all those monsters in the ocean.

Two middle-class GIRLS *enter*

FIRST GIRL

What lovely fabrics! And the jewellery!

SECOND GIRL

Some kind admirer might make us a gift.

FIRST GIRL

If they buy gifts today it's sure to be
For dubious, disgusting motives. Ugh!

SECOND GIRL

Not even then, my dear. Their taste is poor.
They're ruined by caviar and the common whore.

FIRST GIRL

That's why they're too arrogant to care
For girls like us.

SECOND GIRL

Or much too shy to dare.

They go.
Under the shadow of a tree drinks are being served to rowdy WORKMEN *who*

are sitting round a table. Music and dancing in the background. Soldiers, bour-
geois and other miscellaneous people are strolling about, enjoying themselves

INNKEEPER
among his customers

Drink up, my lads, don't mourn for yesterday,
Tomorrow is a shore man never reaches,
The Lord provides for all his little sparrows,
And all is vanity, the good book teaches.

LUCIFER

Now this philosophy appeals to me.
Let's take a seat on this nice shady bench
And see how cheaply men amuse themselves
With sour wine and a bit of jangling music.

FIRST WORKMAN
at the table

I tell you those machines are devil's work,
They snatch the bread out of our very mouths.

SECOND WORKMAN

As long as there's enough to drink, forget them.

FIRST WORKMAN

It's those devils, the rich, who suck our blood.
If a rich man turned up now I'd give him hell.
We should take action, like we did before.

THIRD WORKMAN

What use is that? You'd hang before the day
Was out, and we'd go on the same old way.

SECOND WORKMAN

What idle talk, so let the rich man come—
I wouldn't fight, I'd sit him down beside me—
We'd soon see who could drink the other under.

INNKEEPER
to ADAM

What can I fetch you, sir?

ADAM

Why, nothing, thank you.

INNKEEPER

Off with you then, you pair of good-for-nothings!
Or do you think I live on stolen earnings,
Or that my wife and kids should go out begging?

ADAM
rising

How dare you, sir?

LUCIFER

Ignore the guttersnipe!

ADAM

Let's go—why should we waste our time observing
Mankind degenerating into brutes.

LUCIFER

But this is what I've looked for all these years,
A place where we could have a splendid time.

179

The din of merriment, abandoned laughter,
The kindling of the Bacchanalian fire
To bring a rosy glow to every cheek,
And lend a foolish mask to poverty.
Isn't it splendid?

ADAM

No, it makes me sick.

In the meantime they have reached a group of dancers. Two BEGGARS
approach quarrelling

FIRST BEGGAR

It's my pitch this, I've got a licence for it.

SECOND BEGGAR

Have pity on me or I die. It's over
A fortnight since I lost my steady job.

FIRST BEGGAR

In that case you can't be a genuine beggar.
Be off, you bungler, or I call the law.

The SECOND BEGGAR *slinks away. The* FIRST BEGGAR *takes up his position*

Alms for Christ's sake and His sacred wounds,
Give alms, good masters, to the suffering!—

An APPRENTICE *is dancing with a* GIRL. *A nearby* SOLDIER *pulls her away
from him*

SOLDIER

Be off, you peasant! Do you fancy yourself
As something special?

APPRENTICE

You might be right, at that.
You might find out.

SECOND APPRENTICE

Don't touch him. Let him be.
He has the lot, the power and the glory.

FIRST APPRENTICE

But why drive home the point with such contempt?
Hasn't the leech sucked too much blood already?

A WHORE
singing

The golden apple had been won
From the dragon long ago,
On trees a thousand apples grow
But where have all the dragons gone?
You're crazy if you stand and stare
Too scared to grab what's hanging there.

She rubs herself against a young man

LUCIFER
absorbed by the sight of the merriment

You see I like this piece of coquetry.
The rich man should display his store of riches.
A trunk of gold might just as well be sand
If a miser only sits on it all day.
How moving is this puppy's jealousy!
And how he hangs on the girl's every glance
He feels the glory of the passing minute,
Although he knows—but oh, why should he care—
That soon she'll be in someone else's arms.

ADAM
to one of the MUSICIANS

Why do you waste your talent on this rubbish!
Tell me, do you like what you are playing?

MUSICIAN

Like it? Good Heavens, no! It's endless torture
Grinding out this stuff from day to day,
To see men dance and hear them bawl for more.
This awful racket even haunts my dreams.
But what can I do? How else can I live?

LUCIFER
still absorbed by the surrounding activity

Ah, who would have imagined giddy youth
Was capable of such philosophy?—
This girl here knows the present hour of pleasure
Is far from being the last one of her life,
While she embraces one man her eyes seek
Some new adventure—Ah, my precious children;
You've no idea how gratifying this is!
That you should labour for me with a smile!
I bless you all with sin and poverty.

SECOND APPRENTICE
singing

A worker when his week is done
Will sing and dance both night and morn,
He'll kiss the girls, go on the booze,
And laugh Old Nick himself to scorn.

We hear the closing bars of a hymn. EVE, *a respectable middle-class girl,
leaves the church with her* MOTHER. *She is holding a prayer-book and
a bunch of flowers*

First Salesman

Just take a look at this, my dear young lady!
You won't find better prices anywhere.

Second Salesman

Don't you believe it, he will sell you short,
His goods are second rate. Step this way, lady!

Adam

Ah Lucifer! Just look, while you insist
On wasting our time in this squalid place
The figure of Salvation passes by!

Lucifer

It wouldn't be the first time that has happened.—

Adam

She has just come from the church, how sweet, how lovely!

Lucifer

She went there to be seen, perhaps to see.

Adam

Keep your icy cynical hands off her.
Beatitude still sits upon her lips.

Lucifer

You're a convert, I see—a real pietist.

ADAM

You miss the point, my own heart may be cold
But that's my business: for her sake I would wish
Her maiden heart to overrun with faith,
With sacred verse, the music of the past
And all the immaculate virgin bloom of flowers.

LUCIFER

Which one is she, show me this piece of heaven—
Even the devil cannot be expected
To know your preferences all the time,
Enough that he allows you to possess them.

ADAM

Oh how could it be anyone but her?

LUCIFER

So speaks the woodpecker who finds a worm,
He looks about suspiciously, believing
That he has caught the tastiest of titbits
While all the time the dove looks on disgusted.
So each man finds his own peculiar
Salvation—often on the very spot
His friends played havoc with and left to rot.

ADAM

What dignity, what chastity, what virtue;
I hardly dare address myself to her.

LUCIFER

Come now, you're no novice with the women,
If we look carefully we'll find her price.

ADAM

Be quiet!

LUCIFER

Though she might be too expensive.

A YOUTH *shyly approaches* EVE *and offers her a piece of gingerbread*

YOUTH

Young lady, be so kind as to accept
This sweetmeat from my hand: it bears my heart.

EVE

How kind, dear Arthur, to remember me.

MOTHER

How long since we last met; why don't you visit?

They talk quietly. ADAM *watches them excitedly, until the* YOUTH *leaves*

ADAM

Can this mere youth accomplish that which I,
A full grown man, vainly desire to do?—
How intimate they are, and how she smiles—
And waves to him—what suffering, what torture!
I've got to speak to her.

He approaches EVE

MOTHER

Well, Arthur's parents
Are wealthy enough, it's true, but I don't know
How they regard his friendship with you, dear.

Take care not to discourage other suitors—
Like that boy who sent you flowers just this morning.

ADAM

Ladies, do allow me to escort you,
And shield you from the milling of the crowd.

EVE

Impertinence!

MOTHER

Be off, importunate!
Or do you think my daughter is the sort
That men can proposition in broad daylight?

ADAM

How else to talk to her? I've often dreamed
Of this most perfect, loveliest of women.

MOTHER

Your dreams are your affair, dream what you like;
My daughter's charms are not intended
For ragamuffins such as you, my man.—

ADAM *stands confused while a* GYPSY WOMAN *approaches* EVE

GYPSY WOMAN

Ah precious lady, world's delight,
Show your tiny hand so white.
Your happy fate you may behold,
And gild your life a thousandfold.

Looking at her palms

I see a handsome husband—wealth,
A host of children, and sound health.

They give her money

LUCIFER
pointing to ADAM

Cousin, do tell us something of my friend.—

GYPSY WOMAN

I can't see clearly—hunger or the rope.

ADAM
to EVE

I beg you, don't dismiss me from your presence,
I feel your heart was made to join with mine.

EVE

Mother, you cannot permit this—

MOTHER

Go away,

Or I'll call the police.

EVE

Don't harm him—perhaps
He'll come to his senses. He has committed no crime.

They hurry away

ADAM

O poetry, are you to disappear
Completely from this too prosaic world?

LUCIFER

By no means! Why, what is this gingerbread,
This bunch of flowers, this dancing and this garden
But poetry? Be less choosy: you'll find
Dream-fodder enough to occupy your mind.

ADAM

What use is that when opportunism
And greed lurk in their midst, when selflessness
And nobility are nowhere to be found.

LUCIFER

They still exist at school, in the old classroom,
The life there is not all economy,
Not yet. And look, here come a few such lads.

A few SCHOLARS *come strolling by*

FIRST SCHOLAR

Cheer up lads, now for some fun.
No more chalk dust, school is done.

SECOND SCHOLAR

But not in town. I do hate all
Its rules and shops and tradesman's stalls.

THIRD SCHOLAR

Let's pick a fight with someone then.
It's more exciting—live like men!

FIRST SCHOLAR

Let's make off with the soldiers' whores.
We'll steal them from their very laps
And straightaway we'll have a war.
Then cut across the fields. Perhaps
We'll have enough for drinks and dances,
And for a while we'll live like princes
Among flushed faces, with the memory
Of our battles and our victory.

FOURTH SCHOLAR

Brilliant, shock the philistines.

FIRST SCHOLAR

Like soldiers we'll enforce our lines,
It's right for us to have our fling,
Before, in due time, we take wing—
Our energies then, like as not,
Will turn us into patriots.

They hurry away

ADAM

There's a fine sight in a world gone flat,
I feel it holds the germ of better times.

LUCIFER

You'll soon see what becomes of that small germ
Once it has shaken off the classroom dust.

Two industrialists are approaching.
They were much the same as those lads in their youth.

Two INDUSTRIALISTS *approach, conversing*

FIRST INDUSTRIALIST

It's quite impossible, I can't compete,
Since everyone demands the cheapest goods,
I'll have to drop the quality of my produce.

SECOND INDUSTRIALIST

We'll have to lower the workers' rates of pay.

FIRST INDUSTRIALIST

It can't be done, they're all still up in arms,
Saying they can't afford to live, the dogs;
There may well be a spark of truth in that,
But after all, who told them to get married,
Who tells them to get half a dozen children?

SECOND INDUSTRIALIST

Then we must take a firmer grip on them
They should labour in the plant for half the night
And find the other half quite rest enough,
Since dreaming for their kind serves little purpose.

They go

ADAM

Away with them!—Why did you let me see them.—
And tell me where that girl has disappeared to?—
Show your power now, Lucifer, assist me
And make her listen to me.

LUCIFER

Lucifer's
Power is not to be wasted on such trifles.

ADAM

A trifle to you but the whole world to me.

LUCIFER

Then so be it, go win her, but control
Your feelings, don't be afraid of lying, speak
As I prompt you and she'll soon be in your arms.

Aloud, so that the GYPSY WOMAN *listening behind them should hear*

And so you see, my lord, how inadvisable
It is to go disguised among the people,
At every turn we meet with some new insult,
If only these men knew four of our ships
Have but today returned from India,
They'd treat you differently.

ADAM

Yes, I suppose so.

GYPSY WOMAN
aside

This nugget should be worth a pretty penny.

to ADAM

A word with you—you came disguised and so
I punished you with forecasts of ill fortune,
Since, as you know, you cannot keep a secret
From one who is an old chum of the devil.

191

LUCIFER
aside

You're all I need, you ancient harridan!

GYPSY WOMAN

Those ships of yours arrive this very day,
But what is cause for even greater pleasure,
A beautiful girl is pining for your love.

ADAM

And how should I win her?

GYPSY WOMAN

Why, she's yours already.

ADAM

She turned me away?

GYPSY WOMAN

That's just why she'll be yours.
You'll see, she'll come back in a little while.
Remember then the fortune-teller's words.

She leaves

ADAM

Lucifer, this old girl will outflank you.

LUCIFER

I'll not dispute her shining attributes,
For now she can play devil's substitute.—

192

QUACK-DOCTOR

Get out of my way—I demand respect,
This head of mine has grown grey in pursuit
Of knowledge, in the ceaseless quarrying
Of nature's hidden secrets.

ADAM

                    Who is this
Remarkable popinjay, Lucifer?

LUCIFER

Science, who has turned showman to survive,
The very science you studied in the past,
Now needs to make a rather louder noise.

ADAM

I never went to such extremes as this.
Shame on him!

LUCIFER

            It's not the fellow's fault,
He is afraid and would prefer to save
Himself that old inscription on one's grave:
    Ex gratia speciali
    Mortuus in hospitali.
Since he has sacrificed both day and night
To others, he must have earned some small respite.

193

QUACK-DOCTOR

Labouring long for the benefit of mankind,
Behold, I bring you the fruits of my physic:
This little phial contains the true elixir
Which restores the youth of the aged and the sick.
The very drug the pharaohs used to swear by,
Tancred's magic potion, Helen's balm
That made her beautiful, and Kepler's secret
Gleaned from the fateful stars and his own palm.

ADAM

Do you hear what he is selling? The light we sought
In years to come he seeks in days gone by.

LUCIFER

The present age never receives due honour:
As in his bedroom no man's fame bears study,
It's like the wife we wed ten years ago,
We've counted every blemish on her body.

QUACK-DOCTOR

Come buy, whoever buys, you won't regret it,
If you don't buy it now you might not get it.

A VOICE IN THE CROWD

Whatever it is, it will do quite nicely.—
What luck. I'll buy it, even though it's pricy.

LUCIFER

You see these people—sceptics to a man,
And yet they'll grab what miracles they can.

EVE *returns with her* MOTHER, *the* GYPSY WOMAN *follows them
whispering*

Eve

Your words are useless: we know what you are.

Gypsy Woman

So curse me heaven if I tell a lie.
This nobleman is so in love with you
He'd take you for his mistress straightaway.
You'd live like a princess, with coach and four
To gallop you to dances or a play.

Mother

Just think of it, it's certainly much better
Than mouldering away one's married life
In some evil smelling, filthy, cobbler's shop.

Gypsy Woman

And there he is—just look, he's searching for you.

Eve

It's annoying that he hasn't noticed me.—
His hands are elegant, his posture noble.—

Mother

Even his friend looks quite acceptable,
His nose is hooked, his legs are bandy, true.
But so respectable, a man of mature years.—
I'll go now, dear. You'll get on so much better
If I leave you two alone a little while.

Gypsy Woman
to Adam

Here is the girl, see how she sighs for you.—

195

ADAM

I'll fly to her—what pleasure, oh what pleasure!

GYPSY WOMAN

But sir, you'll not forget your go-between.

LUCIFER
paying her

The money is my friend's, the handshake mine.

GYPSY WOMAN
screaming out

Aah, what a grip you have!

She goes

LUCIFER

     How pleased you'd be
If you were what you claimed, you withered hag!

EVE
to ADAM

You could buy me a little present if you liked,
That nice cosmetic lotion offered there.—

ADAM

Your face embodies all a woman's charms,
And no cosmetic lotion could match that.

The QUACK-DOCTOR *departs as they talk*

EVE

Ah, you are generous.

ADAM

Don't embarrass me:
I'll drape your lovely neck with pearls and diamonds,
But not in order to embellish it;
They could not gleam in a more perfect setting.—

EVE

I saw a lot of jewellers down there,
But they are not for poor girls such as I.

ADAM

Well, let us see them.

LUCIFER

There's no need for that,
It so happens I have some fine gems with me.

He hands over some jewellery which EVE *examines and tries out with great happiness*

EVE

How kind, how lovely, my friends will be so jealous.

ADAM
pointing to the heart-shaped biscuit given by the youth

But not this heart—let's see no more of it.

EVE

I'll throw the thing away if it offends you.

She throws the heart down

LUCIFER

Quite right, I'll step on it.

He grinds it under heel

EVE

What's that:
I heard a scream, or did I fancy it?

As she speaks a condemned man is carried across the stage on a cart, the crowd jostling in its wake

VOICES FROM THE CROWD

Hurry up.—I told you he was windy.—
He's still struggling.—Get up and follow him!

ADAM

What is all this crush and noise about?

EVE

A hanging. We are lucky to be here.
Let's follow them, it's such a thrilling sight,
It'll give me a chance to show the pearls off too.

ADAM

What has the scoundrel done?

EVE

I've no idea.

198

LUCIFER

It doesn't really matter but I'll tell you:
He worked for years in Lovel's factory,
But lead is poison and he would inhale it
And while he spent some weeks in hospital,
His pretty little wife fell on hard times,
And Lovel's son being young and generous,
They found each other and forgot their troubles.—

FIRST WORKMAN

Cheerly old mate!—You'll die a martyr's death,
And we will keep your reputation shining.

LUCIFER

The man recovered, couldn't find his wife,
His post was filled, he couldn't get another,
He grew hot tempered, dared to utter threats,
Then Lovel's son slapped him across the face.
The poor wretch seized a knife that lay close by—
And there he goes—old Lovel lost his senses.—

And as he speaks, LOVEL *appears, half crazed with grief*

LOVEL

You lie, you lie, it's not I who is mad,
Do I not hear my son's wounds whispering?
Take it, take all of it, my endless wealth,
I'd rather not hear. I'd sooner lose my reason!

THIRD WORKMAN
to the condemned man

Courage, the day of reckoning will come.

FIRST WORKMAN

Go with raised head, they are the guilty ones.—

The condemned man leaves with his retinue

ADAM

The sight freezes my marrow, why does it haunt me?
Who could tell here who is more to blame?
Perhaps the sin lies with society;
Once that begins to rot, vice spreads like fungus.

LOVEL

Society, that's it!—Take all my money,
As long as I don't have to hear those wounds.—

He goes

EVE

Come on, come on, or we won't find a place.

ADAM

I thank my lucky stars that I'm no judge.
It's easy to write laws in easy chairs—
It's easy to pass judgment from on high,
But how much harder to explore the heart
Or fairly analyse its dark procedures.

LUCIFER

Such principles would make for endless trials.
No one does wrong simply because it's wrong,
Even the devil has his alibi,
And each man thinks his own the most important.
A good solicitor can cut the knots
That do-gooders are incapable of slipping.

Meanwhile they have reached The Tower, in a recess of which is the image of a saint

EVE

May we pause here just a little while?
I'd like to place my flowers on this shrine.

LUCIFER
in an undertone

Don't, don't let her, or we shall be lost.

ADAM

The harmless child—I won't stand in her way.—

EVE

I used to pray here when I was a child,
Whenever I pass it I remember this
And say a prayer—it is a source of pleasure.—
I'll only be a moment, and if we hurry
We'll make up the lost time.

She pins the flowers beside the picture, but they suddenly wither and the jewels on her arm and neck turn to serpents, uncoil and fall to the ground

My God, what's this?

LUCIFER

I warned you but you didn't listen.

EVE

Help!

ADAM

Calm down, my dear, or everyone will notice—
Your neck will hang with jewels a thousandfold.

EVE

Away from me! O help, have mercy on me!
God help me, I'm an honest girl! That hag
And those two conjurors have brought me to this.

A crowd gathers around them, and the GYPSY WOMAN *returns with some*
policemen

GYPSY WOMAN

They must be here, they paid me in false coin,
It started melting in my hand.

LUCIFER

Perhaps
The fault lay in your palm, not in the coins.—
Let's go Adam, it's no fun being here.

They disappear into The Tower, and while the disturbance grows below
they appear once more upon the battlements

ADAM

More disillusion, I thought it was enough
To topple the grim idols of the past
And give our energies a freer rein.—
I threw away the central mechanism
Which held the works together—reverence—
And neglected to replace it with one stronger.
What contest can it be when an armed man
Confronts opponents who are bare and forked?
What independence when a hundred starve
Unless they bear some individual's yoke?
It's worse than dogs fighting for a bone.
I'd have a society which protects
Not punishes, exhorts not terrifies,
Which gains its strength from common enterprise,
One conceived by science to please itself,

A system which the intellect has ordered.—
And this will come to be, I feel and know it,
O lead me, Lucifer, lead me to this world.—

LUCIFER

How vain you are. Because your feeble sight
Only allows you glimpses of confusion
You think there is no underlying order,
No system in the engine room of life?
Just look now through the eyes these spirits lend you
And see the work they're bringing to completion
Not for themselves, poor fellows, but for us.

*It grows dark. The whole market seems to form one group, digging a grave in
the centre of the stage, dancing round it, and one after another leaping into it,
some silently, others after delivering brief speeches*

CHORUS

Dig on, the work must be complete
Before the rising sun,
Although a thousand years may pass
And leave the bulk undone.
The cradle and the grave are one
And end what they begin,
Hungry yet full, they raise today
Those yesterday thrown in!

The angelus rings out

The angelus resounds, pack up,
Go home and go to bed,
Those whom dawn awakes can face
The work that remains ahead

PUPPETEER

My japes are done, I've played my part,
Amused the world, left unamused my heart.

INNKEEPER

The ale is drunk and all are tight,
Goodnight, sweet customers, goodnight.

FLOWER GIRL

I've sold what violets I have,
But fresh ones blossom on my grave.

GYPSY WOMAN

Men long to see the future clear,
But now they close their eyes in fear.

LOVEL

My wealth brought only misery,
This new tranquility comes free.

WORKMAN

The week is done, it's Saturday,
My daily pains are soothed away.

SCHOLAR

My dreams were sweet—my waking rough,
I'll start again where they left off.

SOLDIER

I thought I was the plucky sort,
But this foul ditch has caught me short.—

WHORE

All passion spent, my skin stripped bare
I feel cold: what's it like down there?

THE CONDEMNED MAN

The chains remain, my clay is poor,
New laws may lie beyond the door.

QUACK-DOCTOR

We each claimed wisdom as our own
But truth astounds all once it's known.

EVE

Why stand there, pit, gaping at my feet!
O never think your night can frighten me:
My dust flies downward, clay returns to clay,
But I shall pass beyond you gloriously.
The soul of passion, poetry and youth
Shall lead me on to the eternal places;
All earth can know of joy is in my smile,
Whose beam of sunlight rests on chosen faces.

She casts her veil and cloak into the grave and rises transfigured

LUCIFER

You recognize her, Adam?

ADAM

Eve! It's Eve!

SCENE 12

The U-shaped courtyard of a majestic Phalanstery. The ground floor of the two wings reveals open colonnaded halls. The one on the right side contains workmen attending vast whirling machines. The one on the left is a museum filled with a remarkable number of scientific instruments associated with chemistry, physics, astronomy, and natural history. A Scientist is working amongst them. Everything and everyone here is a part of the Phalanstery. All are dressed alike. Adam and Lucifer rise from the middle of the courtyard floor. It is day.

ADAM

Where are we now? What land or nation is this?

LUCIFER

Those old ideas have vanished. Don't you think
That nationalism was a petty concept?
Prejudice gave it birth, and rivalry
And narrow-mindedness were its defence.
The whole world is a single nation now,
With all men working to a common purpose,
And above this tranquil stream that flows to order,
Revered by all, the scientist stands guard.

ADAM

All that I dreamt of is fulfilled at last.
Now everything is as I wanted it.
I've one regret: the nationhood ideal,
Which could have survived and been adapted to
The scheme of things, even as they stand.
Our souls need limits, fear the infinite,
Scattered too wide they lose the power within;
They cling to everything, the past, the future;
I fear too big a world will not be loved
As much as the soil in which our parents lie.
A man who'd shed his blood to save his children
Will shed but tears at best for mere acquaintance.

LUCIFER

You shun the objects you idealized
Even before they could be realized.

ADAM

That is not true. But I am curious:
What ideal is this that welds together
The whole world; that shapes the everlasting
Fire of human souls—that enthusiasm
Fanned, corrupted, time and time again,
Diverted by imaginary struggles—
And drives it to some nobler end at last.—
But tell me first, where are we, in what place?
Then lead me on, and let my soul enjoy
The thought that after countless years of struggle
Man has finally gained his just reward.

LUCIFER

This phalanstery is one of a great number,
A home for those imbued with new ideals.—

ADAM

Then let us go.

LUCIFER

                No, not so fast. Just wait.
Before we do, we have to change our form.
If we appeared as Lucifer and Adam
No man of science would believe in us,
They'd kill us or imprison us in test tubes.

ADAM

What nonsense you do talk from time to time.

LUCIFER

There's no way but this in the spirit world.

ADAM

Then go ahead, do what you want, but quickly.

LUCIFER *alters their shapes so that they look like members of the*
Phalanstery

LUCIFER

Here, put on this outfit. Off with your locks—
Now we are ready.—

ADAM

Let's speak to this scientist.

LUCIFER

Good afternoon, professor!

SCIENTIST

Don't disturb me
At my work. I've no time for mere chatter.

LUCIFER

I do apologize. We're delegates
From Phalanstery One Thousand, on observation,
It was your fame that brought us all this way.

SCIENTIST

Your energy does you credit, I admit.
Well, maybe I could leave my work a while;
Providing the alembics don't cool down
The material remains quite tractable.

LUCIFER
aside

It's as I thought, even you, who have filtered
Mankind and nature through your intellect
Have retained your residue of vanity.

SCIENTIST

So now we can relax a little while.—
What is your field of specialization?

ADAM

We're not attached to a particular one
But would prefer to take a general view.

SCIENTIST

You're wrong—great things are hidden in small details.
And life's too short to tackle every subject.

ADAM

That's true—I fully understand we need
Both carriers of sand and hewers of stone:
One cannot build a house without their labour.
But these have only the foggiest idea
Of the grand design in which they play a part.—
Only the architect comprehends the whole,
And even if he cannot carve the stone
The work is his creation, he its god.—
The architect is great in science too.

LUCIFER

And that, great man, is why we come to you.

210

SCIENTIST

You have done well, and I am very flattered.
Science has many fruitful branches, all
Different, yet it owes its charm to their
Organic unity.

LUCIFER

Like a pretty woman.

SCIENTIST

But having said that, it is Chemistry—

LUCIFER

That lies at the centre, at its very heart.

SCIENTIST

Precisely.

LUCIFER

Though a mathematician once said
The same of mathematics.

SCIENTIST

Vanity
Makes everyone the centre of their own
Field of vision.

LUCIFER

But you've done well to choose
Chemistry as your own special study.

SCIENTIST

Of that I have no doubt at all.—But come,
Let us take a look round the museum.
There's not another like it in the world,
You will find every prehistoric creature
Displayed in here, all original samples,
And finely mounted.—Thousands of them dwelt
Among our ancestors in darker times,
Sharing dominion with them as it were.—
There are many fantastic stories about them,
Take this example, once used as a train.

ADAM

That is a *horse*. Of a degenerate breed
The Arab steed was quite a different matter.

SCIENTIST

They say that man would keep these as a friend,
Without regard to profit nor expecting
Labour from them, and that through close attention
The creature could divine his master's thoughts.
And what is more, they say that he adopted
Man's own vices, the sense of property,
Would even sacrifice his life for it.—
I'm only telling you what's written down,
I don't accept it unconditionally.
They had illusions—many strange ideas,
And this is one that has come down to us.

ADAM

This is a *dog*.—And all you've said is true.

LUCIFER

Beware Adam, you might betray yourself.

SCIENTIST

This creature used to be the poor man's slave.

ADAM

And the poor were yoked like *oxen* to the rich.

SCIENTIST

And this ruled the savannah.

ADAM

                  It's a *lion.*
And look, here is a tiger, and a deer.
What creatures are left living in the world?

SCIENTIST

What can you mean? Is it different where you are?
What lives is what is useful or what science
Has found no adequate substitute for yet
Like pigs and sheep, but not in the poor state
The nature so ineptly left them in.
One's living fat, the other meat and wool,
They serve our needs, exactly like these test-tubes.
I see that you're acquainted with all this,
Consider something else then. For example
Our minerals: this giant lump of coal.
There used to be whole mountains of the stuff
That man could gather up with his bare hands
And now we have to take great pains to filter
It from the air. This metal here is iron,
And while it lasted we did not have to search
For aluminium. This tiny chunk is gold.
It was highly valued and absolutely useless.
When man was blind and worshipped higher beings
Above even the reach of fate, he would
Attribute similar powers to this same gold,

213

And sacrifice his comforts and his rights
Upon its altar so as to obtain
Some tiny morsel of the magic substance,
In exchange for which he could get everything,—
Yes, even bread, amazingly enough.

ADAM

Come, show me something else, I know all this.

SCIENTIST

You must be a most learned fellow, stranger.
All right then, let's examine some old plants.
Now this rose was the very last to bloom
On earth. The thing had no discernible function,
One of a thousand that took the nourishment
Required by fields of corn; the favourite plaything
Of grown up children. It is indeed peculiar
That people should have cared for such a toy;
The very soul of man bore flowers of sorts
In images of poetry and faith.
And men would dissipate their energy,
Neglect the aim and purpose of their lives
To dally with such false and idle dreams.
We have preserved as representative
Two curious works. The first one is poem:
Its author, culpable of the desire
For individual fame, was known as Homer.
He describes in it a quite fantastic world
Which he calls Hades. We long ago disproved
His every line. The other document
Is *Agricola,* the author Tacitus.
It is a quaint and yet regrettable
Account of life in the barbaric world.

ADAM

So there remain at least a few stray leaves
Of those great ages, like a testament,
And I suppose they are incapable
Of inciting their degenerate descendants
To rebel against this artificial world?

SCIENTIST

An acute remark. We have foreseen all this,
We know the hidden poison is most dangerous,
And that's why men are not allowed to read it
Until they have passed sixty years of age
And pledged their lives to the strict pursuit of science.

ADAM

But wouldn't nursery songs and fairy tales
Infect an infant mind with fantasy?

SCIENTIST

Your observation is correct and so
Our nurses' stories are about equations,
Diagrams and geometrical figures.

ADAM
aside

You murderers, do you not go in fear
Of robbing the infant of his precious childhood!

SCIENTIST

Let us proceed.—These are the instruments.
The articles are most amazing shapes.
This is a cannon: it bears a cryptic motto:
Ultima ratio regum.—How it was used

Is a mystery. And this thing is a sword,
It can only have been used for homicide,—
And those who killed with it were not thought criminals.
This picture here was drawn by hand alone—
It might have taken half a lifetime's work,
And note its subject, an eccentric story.
But nowadays the sunlight is enough
And captures not some false idealization
But images both true and functional.

ADAM
aside

But all the art and spirit have departed.

SCIENTIST

These various objects—how gaudy they all are,
How infantile. This goblet with a flower,
This chairback with its fancy arabesques,
Are examples of their wasted manual work.
Is water more refreshing from that glass,
Or is the chair more comfortable to sit on?
Today machines can make these things for us
In their simplest and most economical forms
And so from such perfection it must follow
That the artisan who makes the nuts and bolts
Is bound to the machine throughout his life.

ADAM

That's why there is no life, no character,
No thought of excellence in anything.—
How then can strength and intellect discover
Occasions to prove their pedigree divine?
Should man desire to struggle and explore
This regulated, ordered universe,
He couldn't even experience the joys
Of danger, since no predators remain.

I see that even science proves a cheat:
Instead of happiness I find a boring
Kindergarten. Not what I expected.

SCIENTIST

Is comradeship not an established fact?
What do men lack for their material welfare?
Really, these thoughts deserve strict punishment.

ADAM

At least inform me what ideal it is
That breathes the unity into such people,
And rouses them to this communal effort.

SCIENTIST

The ideal that binds our people is subsistence.
When humankind first came upon the scene
It found a well-stocked larder at its disposal:
Man only needed to extend his hand
To gather all he needed, fit for use.
And so he squandered all, without a thought,
Like maggots in the cheese, and in his stupor
Found time to dabble in romantic theories
And seek out stimulants and poetry.
But we, who are left with the last crumbs of cheese,
We must be prudent, since we've known for years
That our supplies are low and we might starve.
The sun will cool down in four thousand years,
The earth will yield no vegetation then;
And so we have but these four thousand years
To find something to take the place of sunlight,
And I believe our scientists can do it.
For heat we could use water—oxidized,
It is the finest heat-retaining substance.
The very secrets of the organism
Are waiting, almost ready to be used.—

I'm glad our interview has led us here.
I had quite forgotten the state of my alembic,
Since I am working on this very problem.

ADAM

Man has grown old indeed if he relies
On test-tubes for assistance in his business.—
But even if his work should prove successful
What monstrous life is this, no voice for thought,
Affections all unfocussed, without object.
An existence that is quite unnatural
Without antithesis, without connection,
In which the individual finds no scope.
Then what remains to mark its character,
Deprived of outside influence, of pain,
Its consciousness bred in a narrow glass?

SCIENTIST

Just look, look how it boils, look how it glows,
Ephemeral forms are jostling in the jar,
It's warm for them in that tight-stoppered space,
Chemical affinities, reactions,
Will all combine together, and the matter
Submit to me, and do just as I say.

LUCIFER

You do amaze me! One thing I can't grasp:
That's how you would prevent reactive matter
From reacting and the non-reactive kind
From not reacting.

SCIENTIST

        What nonsense you do speak;
That's the eternal law of elements.

LUCIFER

Ah, now I see, but tell me how you know this?

SCIENTIST

How? That is the law, that's how it is.
Experience has clearly borne it out.

LUCIFER

So you are only nature's boilerman,
She can manage the rest all by herself.—

SCIENTIST

But I can shape her laws with my alembic,
And call them from their obscure hiding-places.

LUCIFER

Well, *I* don't see much sign of life in there.

SCIENTIST

It won't be long now. I, who have observed
Every secret of the organism,
Dissected life a hundred times or more—

ADAM

Have every time discovered it a corpse.
Science can only lamely hobble after
Experience which is forever young,
And like the king's official laureate
Is happy enough to sing of what is passing
But is not in the business of telling people's fortunes.

SCIENTIST

But why this sarcasm? Can't you two see
It only needs a spark to spring to life.

ADAM

A spark indeed, but where is it to come from?

SCIENTIST

It can only be a step away, no more.

ADAM

But if a person fails to take that step
He has done nothing, and what he knows is nothing.
Everything else is there, out in the yard,
It needs but this to lead him to the sanctum.—
But when will anyone perform this feat?

*While they speak the smoke from the alembic grows thicker and begins to
rumble*

THE VOICE OF THE SPIRIT OF THE EARTH
from the smoke

No-one. Never.—This tube is both too spacious,
And too tight for me. You recognize me, Adam,
Do you not—though they will not suspect it.

ADAM

Oh did you hear the voice of the great spirit?
Oh look, look there, you proud and feeble creature,
How could you cope with that which floats before you?—

SCIENTIST

The man has had a brainstorm. I fear for you!

The alembic cracks, the SPIRIT *disappears*

The glass has cracked. I'll have to start again
From the beginning. While the goal still beckons
The tiniest thing, some particle, some chance,
Can ruin things.

LUCIFER

That used to be called Fate,
And it was considered less disgraceful then
To break beneath it than it is to yield
To accident now.

The sound of a bell

What does that bell mean?

SCIENTIST

A well-earned rest. It's time to take a walk,
The workers leave their factories and fields,
Now those who have done something wrong are punished,
Women and children are distributed.
Let's go there—I have business there myself.

A long queue of men appears, another of women, some of them with children.
EVE *is among them. They all form a circle in the courtyard and an* ELDER *takes*
his place before them. ADAM, LUCIFER *and the* SCIENTIST *stand in the fore-*
ground next to the Museum

ELDER

Number Thirty!

LUTHER
stepping forward

Present.

ELDER

Once again
The furnace has been wildly overheated.
It seems to us that your enthusiasm
Is beginning to threaten the whole Phalanstery.

LUTHER

Who could resist temptation while that fierce
Element crackles, spits and bellows,
Encircling you with thousands of bright tongues
That leap towards you, hoping to destroy you:
To stand before it bravely, fanning it,
Knowing full well that you are in control—
You cannot know the magic power of fire
If you've only seen it warm a frying pan.

ELDER

Vainglorious talk—no supper for you today.

LUTHER
returning to the ranks

But I will fan the fire again tomorrow.

ADAM

What's this I see? I recognize the man.
That was Luther.

ELDER

Two hundred and nine!

CASSIUS
stepping forward

Present.

ELDER

It is the third time we have spoken
About your fighting without provocation.

CASSIUS

No provocation? Am I not provoked?—
Those fit enough to stand up for themselves
Are cowards if they squeal for help. Was he
So feeble then as not to stay and fight?

ELDER

None of your cheek. Your noble skull has not
Prevented you from harbouring bad instincts.
Your blood is much too hot and turbulent!
Until you calm down we shall have to treat you.

ADAM

Ah Cassius, if you could recognize me,
Your comrade at Philippi. Is this system
So corrupt, this theory so misguided
That a noble heart like yours is seen to be
Nothing but an undistinguished nuisance?

ELDER

Four hundred! Step forward.

PLATO
stepping forward

Yes, I heard you.

ELDER

You're lost in dreams again, and so the cattle
You were supposed to tend have come to harm.
To wake you up we'll make you kneel on grain.

PLATO
returning to the ranks

My dreams are sweet, even on hard grains.

ADAM

Ah Plato, what a role they've given you,
And this in the society you coveted.

ELDER

Seventy-two, step forward!

MICHELANGELO
stepping forward

                              Here I am.

ELDER

You've left your workplace in a dreadful mess.

MICHELANGELO

Yes, because I'm always making chair legs,
And what is more, they are the ugliest shapes.
I've often enough begged to change the form,
To be allowed to carve some new design.
You wouldn't let me. I asked, for a change,
To work on the chairback—that was all in vain.
And I was on the verge of madness when
I left that torture chamber called the workshop.

He returns to the ranks

ELDER

This breach of order means you are confined
Within your room. You'll do without your sunlight.

ADAM

Ah, Michelangelo, what hell it is
For a demigod not to be creative.—
How many well-known faces everywhere,
How many souls, how many ancient powers.
One fought beside me, another died a martyr,
This one thought the whole wide world too narrow,
But how the state has ground down everyone
To dwarfish uniformity. Oh Lucifer,
Let's go—my soul has had enough of this.

ELDER

Today two children have outgrown the age
When they require a mother's full attention,
They must be transferred to the nursery,
So come along now.

EVE *and another woman step forward with their children*

ADAM

          What a glorious sight!
So even this cold world is not devoid
Of poetry!

LUCIFER

Are we going or not?

ADAM

No, there is no better place than this.

ELDER

Doctor, examine the phrenology
Of these children.

The SCIENTIST *examines their skull formation*

EVE

What will become of me.

ADAM

That voice!

LUCIFER

A common woman. What is she
To you who've tasted Semiramis' kisses?

ADAM

But then I did not know her.

LUCIFER

Oh, I see!
That is the age old plaint of every lover;
Each of them maintains that he discovered
Passion, and that none before him knew
The true nature of love. So nothing changes.
The same old song persists a thousand years.

SCIENTIST

We'll educate this infant as a doctor.
This one as a shepherd.

ELDER

Off they go then.

They want to take the children away. EVE *opposes them*

EVE

Don't you dare touch them! This child belongs to me:
Who'd want to tear him from his mother's breast!—

ELDER

Take them away, what are you waiting for?

EVE

O my baby! Mine, since I nourished you
With the blood of my own heart.—What earthly power
Would dare to cut that sacramental cord?
Should I surrender you for ever then,
To lose you in the crowd and seek you vainly
With anxious glances, somewhere among a hundred
Anonymous and near-identical strangers?

ADAM

If there is anything that you hold sacred
You must allow this woman to keep her child.

EVE

That's right, that's right, O you blessed stranger.

ELDER

This is a very dangerous game, stranger;
If we allowed the prejudice for families
To survive, we'd sacrifice at once
The benefits of our beloved science.

EVE

But what is it to me, your frosty science!
Let science hold its peace when nature speaks.

ELDER

May we proceed now?

ADAM

Lay no hand on her.
A sword lies there and I will teach you how
To use it.

LUCIFER

Stay, you image from a dream!

He puts his hand on ADAM*'s shoulder.* ADAM *freezes*

Feel the decisive power of my hand.

EVE

Oh my child!

She collapses as her child is taken away

ELDER

These two young women here
Are partnerless. Apply now if you want them.

ADAM

I'll take this one.

ELDER

What do you say, doctor?

SCIENTIST

A fanatic man and an unstable woman
Will breed substandard children. It is wrong.

ADAM

But I will not desert her if she wants me.

EVE

I will be yours, most generous of men.

ADAM

I love you, lady, love you with all my heart.

EVE

I love you too. I feel I've always loved you.

SCIENTIST

This is madness—it's really most disturbing
To see such spectres of the past in this
Enlightened age. Where can they have come from?

ADAM

We are late beams of sunlight out of Eden.

ELDER

That is regrettable.—

ADAM

Don't pity us!
The madness is our own; we are not jealous
Of your sanity, since all outstanding
And noble things in this world have been madness,
And no amount of reason could control them.—
Spirit voices are drifting down to us
From nobler spheres with delicate vibrations,
To show us that our souls are kin to theirs,
So we despise the low dust of the earth
And seek out ways to reach those higher spheres.

He embraces EVE

230

ELDER

Why should we listen to any more of this,
Take them away, down to the hospital.

LUCIFER

You need help quickly, Adam. Let's be going!

They sink into the ground

SCENE 13

*In space. A segment of the Earth is seen in the distance, growing ever smaller,
until it seems as distant as a star, indistinguishable from the others. The scene
begins in a twilight grey, which slowly darkens to pitch black. ADAM is a very
old man. He and LUCIFER are flying through space.*

ADAM

How furiously we have flown. Where are we?

LUCIFER

Did you not wish to rise above the earth
To higher spheres, where, if I understood you
Quite correctly, you have heard the cries
Of fellow spirits?

ADAM

      That is true, but I
Never imagined the way to be so barren.
This world is all so alien and deserted
That to trespass in it seems a sacrilege,
And I am subject to an inner conflict:
I feel the meanness of an Earth that bound
My aspirations, and long to break its hold,
And yet I'm homesick, breaking free is painful.—
Ah Lucifer! Just look back at our planet,
The flowers were first to vanish from our sight,
And then the trembling branches of the forests;
Our well-known haunts, a hundred favourite nooks
Have levelled down, become a featureless plain.
Whatever thrilled us has been washed away.
Now even the cliffs have shrunk to useless clods,
The thunder-bellied cloud which terrifies
Peasants below, who take it for a portent,
Has thinned to a poor drifting shred of vapour.

233

The endless grumbling ocean—where is that?
It sits there like a grey patch on the face
Of one poor planet lost among the others,
And this was once the whole wide world to us.
Oh Lucifer! And then there's her, yes her—
Must she remain below, so far from us?—

LUCIFER

Unfortunately, from this eminence
First the beautiful, and then the noble
And the powerful all fade away, until
Nothing's left but a series of cold figures.—

ADAM

We're leaving the very stars behind us now,
I see no end, I feel no obstacle.
What's life without the striving and the passion?
This deep cold terrifies me, Lucifer!

LUCIFER

If this is the limit of your vaunted courage
We should return to playing in the dust.

ADAM

Who said it was? No, forward, let's go forward:
It only hurts until the ties are broken,
Each web of rope that holds me to the earth.—
But what is this? I find it hard to breathe,
I've little strength, my thoughts are all confused.
The tale that tells how Antaeus could survive
Only until his feet still touched the ground—
Was it more than legend?

The Voice of the Spirit of the Earth

More indeed.
You know me well, the Spirit of the Earth,
It is only I that breathe in you, remember.
Here is the border, the limit of my power,
If you return you live—go on, you perish,
You squirm and wriggle like a worm in water—
That puddle is the whole wide world to you.

Adam

Then I defy you, you have failed to scare me.—
My body may be yours, my soul is mine,
The power of thought and truth is infinite,
And came before this material world of yours.

The Voice of the Spirit of the Earth

Vain man! Attempt it, what a fall awaits you.
Did her fragrance anticipate the rose,
The form the body, the ray of light the sun?
If only you could see your orphaned spirit
Circling through the endlessness of space,
Seeking vainly for a shred of meaning
Or expression in an alien universe,
But understanding nothing, feeling nothing,
You would shudder. And that is because each sense,
Each single feeling you possess is only
An emanation of this core or matter
Which you have called your Earth, which were it different,
Neither you nor it would have existed.
All your ideas of fair or foul, of blessed
Or cursed, you have gleaned from me alone,
It is my soul that permeates the fabric
Of your little world. Oh, what passes here
For eternal truth might be incredible
Elsewhere and the impossible seem natural.
No gravity exists, life does not move,
What here is air might very well be thought,

235

What here is light might over there be sound,
A plant-like growth here, there might be a crystal.

ADAM

You cannot shake me, my spirit will press on.

THE VOICE OF THE SPIRIT OF THE EARTH

Adam, Adam, you have but a few minutes:
Go back, on Earth you might achieve true greatness,
But once you have forced your spirit through the ring
Of all existence, God will not permit you
To approach Him—He will shrink and wreck you.

ADAM

Would earth not also wreck me in the end?—

THE VOICE OF THE SPIRIT OF THE EARTH

Oh not the foolish words of that old lie,
Do not repeat them here among the spirits.—
The whole of nature shivers at the sound.—
That is the sacred hidden seal of God,
Reserved unto Himself. Not even the Fruit
Of The Tree of Knowledge could break that seal.

ADAM

Then I will.

They fly on. ADAM *screams out and freezes*
I have perished!

LUCIFER
cackling

And so the old lie has triumphed.—

He pushes ADAM *away from himself*

This puppet god can now go into orbit
Like a planet on which new life might evolve
All over again to give me fresh employment.—

THE VOICE OF THE SPIRIT OF THE EARTH

You laugh too soon. He merely brushed against
The alien world. It's not so easy to break
The bounds of my realm, Lucifer.—Your home
Is calling you; come to yourself, my son.

ADAM
regaining consciousness

I live again.—I sense because I suffer,
But even suffering is sweet to me,
Annihilation is so horrifying.—
O Lucifer, please lead me back to earth,
There where I've fought so many useless battles,
I'll fight again and that will make me happy.

LUCIFER

So after all these trials you still believe
That these new battles may not be so useless?
That you will reach your goal? Only humanity
Could remain so incorrigibly childish.

ADAM

I'm quite untempted by that foolish prospect,
I know that I will fail and fail again
And I don't care. What other goal is there?
It is the end of an honourable contest,
The goal is death, but life consists of struggle,
The struggle in itself must be the goal.

LUCIFER

Oh what a consolation, if your battle
Were fought for some commensurate ideal,
But what you prize today you'll mock tomorrow,
The cause that fired you then will seem like child's play.—
Did you not bleed at Chaeronea once
Defending the lost cause of liberty,
And later, did you not join Constantine
In order to establish his great empire?
And were you not a martyr for your faith
And later, with the armoury of science,
Oppose the very faith that you had died for?

ADAM

That may be true, and yet however false
Ideals they were, they managed to inspire
And raise me up: they all were great and sacred.
It is all one, whatever form it took,
The Cross or science, liberty, ambition,
They all *advanced* the progress of mankind.—
Oh back to earth, I want to fight again.

LUCIFER

Have you so soon forgot the scientist's words;
Who calculated that the earth would freeze
Four thousand years—putting an end to struggle?

ADAM

If science doesn't challenge that assumption.
But science will, I feel it in my bones.—

LUCIFER

And then?—Will there be battles, greatness, power
In that artificial world the human mind
Created round its tidy theorems,
That world which you observed a while ago?

ADAM

As long as the earth is saved—then it will pass
Like those before, like things that have fulfilled
Their purpose, and once again creative thought
Will re-emerge and breathe life into it.
Take me back now, I'm burning to see what
New doctrine will inspire me in the world
That has been saved.

LUCIFER

Very well then, back.—

SCENE 14

A barren, mountainous landscape, covered in snow and ice. The sun stands still among wreaths of mist, a blood-coloured sphere that gives out no rays. The light is dim. In the foreground we see a few stunted birches, and, between a juniper and a dwarf pine, an Eskimo hut. ADAM, *a broken old man, descends from the hill, with the aid of a walking stick, accompanied by* LUCIFER.

ADAM

Why must we roam this endless world of snow
Where death looks out at us with empty eyes,
And only a seal or two disturbs the silence,
Diving beneath the waves when startled by
Our steps; where even plants are too exhausted
To strive for life and stunted bushes sway
Among the lichen, and the red-faced moon
Glares behind fog like a lantern in a grave?—
Lead me there where palms grow, that paradise
Of sunshine and sweet fragrance, where man's soul
Is fully conscious of its latent power.—

LUCIFER

That's where we are. That ball of blood is your sun.
Directly beneath our feet is the Equator.
Science has finally destroyed itself.

ADAM

A dreadful world!—The best thing is to die.
I won't regret the world I leave behind.
Ah Lucifer! That I who once stood beside
The cradle of humanity and knew
What mighty hopes attended on his rocking,
Who fought beside him in his every battle,
That I should now survey this monstrous grave
Which nature has entangled in her shroud!

241

I, then the first, and now the last of men,
Would like to know the manner of our going.
Did we die bravely, fighting to the last
Or miserably shrink from post to post,
Undignified, unworthy of lament?

LUCIFER

How vain you are about your 'mighty' soul—
As you will keep referring to that power
Which sends the blood careering through the veins,
And swells a young man's breast with high ideals:
Do not desire to linger to the end
As witness at your own death-bed. This is
A marvellous hour for auditing accounts
Prepared in the master's absence. The delirium
Will put to flight the mirages produced
By life's own fever. Who'll know what was real then?
That final feeble rattle in the throat
Is the roar of mockery at all our battles.

ADAM

O why did I not perish at my peak,
In full control of all my faculties,
Body and soul, rather than hear my own
Epitaph indifferently spoken
By one whose spirit is cold, who has no share
In either my battles or in my demise.—

LUCIFER

Again, to me these tears betray your species,
And accompany your waking from a fond
Illusion to the harsh reality.
But rest assured, your species still survives.
Look there, there stands a human habitation,
And see, its owner has just come through the door.

An ESKIMO *steps from his hut, dressed for a seal-hunt*

ADAM

This stunted shape, this strange deformity,
Is he the heir to my estate?
Why show me such things, Lucifer!
The cure is worse than the disease.

ESKIMO

And do the gods still live above?
Here they stand now, in the flesh.
Are they good or evil though?
I'll play it safe and run away.

He makes to flee

LUCIFER

Wait! A word with you!

ESKIMO
falling to his knees

Have mercy on me!
I promise I will sacrifice to you
The first seal that I catch, if you don't hurt me.

LUCIFER

What right have you to sacrifice the life
Of that poor seal in order to save your own?

ESKIMO

Because I'm stronger; I look around
And see the fish consume the worm,
Seal eat the fish, and I the seal.

LUCIFER

And the great spirit in turn will feed on you.

ESKIMO

I know, the little time he lets
Me in his mercy have, I buy
With blood of sacrifice.

ADAM

How cowardly!

LUCIFER

You think you would have acted otherwise?
Between you two there is a single difference:
He sacrifices seals and you live men,
You to a god created in your image
And he to one in his.

ESKIMO

I see you're angry,
I think I know why. In my need
I called the kind god of the sun
Who asks for nothing, but gives all,
And who, as the old stories tell,
Was once the ruler here. But pardon,
I'll curse him for your sake for ever.

ADAM

Behold, O mighty God, look down and blush
To see how wretched man is, he whom You
Intended to be the wonder of the world!—

ESKIMO

Your friend is angry. Is he hungry too?

LUCIFER

It is just because he's not that he is angry.

ADAM

Why must you joke at such an awful time!

LUCIFER

It's no joke but the truth. Your reasoning
Is typical of a full stomach—his
Is the philosophy of one that's empty.
You'll not convince each other with your reasons,
But you would soon see eye to eye with him
If you were hungry or if he had eaten.—
Oh yes, whatever you choose to imagine,
The animal in you takes precedence,
And only once he satisfies the beast
Does man begin contemptuously to think
Of abandoning his primal character.

ADAM

That speech was quite in character for you,
You like debasing all things that are sacred.
So all our high ideals and noble deeds
Are nothing but the steam of primal kitchens,
Or a lumpen sum of circumstantial forces
Disposing every element according
To laws that govern rudimentary matter?

LUCIFER

But are there others? Do you then believe
Leonidas would have perished in the pass

If only instead of supping on brown soup
In a penniless democracy, he'd lounged
In a villa and dabbled in all the pleasures
And intoxications that the East could offer?
Would Brutus have died if he had hurried home
To lovely Portia and after a sound meal
Slept off the hot excitement of his battle?
Where are vice and majesty both bred?
Though one is born in stinking poverty
Another one in sunlight and in freedom,
Do not both perpetuate their character
In spirit and in body through their children?
How many have said they've rendered their accounts
And strung themselves up on a handy branch,
But when some unforeseen blade cut the rope
The new life quickened in them and they left
Accountancy? If Hunyadi were born
Not in his proper home, but found his cradle
Rocked in the shadow of a Saracen tent
Would we have gained the first of Christian heroes?
What if Luther had chanced to be the Pope
And Leo a teacher in a German college:
Who knows, the latter might have turned reformer
And the first cast his anathema against
The turbulent rebel. Take Napoleon,
What if his path had not been straightened by
The blood of a whole nation? He might have
Mouldered away in a stinking barrack-room.—

ADAM
clapping his hand over LUCIFER's *mouth*

Enough!—since every issue you expound
Appears so plain and irrefutable
It's all the more pernicious.—Superstition
Blinds only those fools who in any case
Are blind to the spirit moving in us all;
But finer men might recognize their brothers
If your cold doctrine did not kill them first.—

LUCIFER

Then speak with your fellow here. A little lesson
In self-knowledge will not come amiss.

ADAM

Are many of you living in this district?

ESKIMO

Oh many indeed, more than I could count
On all my fingers. But even though I beat
My neighbours' heads in, it is pointless,
New settlers will keep coming, seals are few.
If god you are, I beg you, do this for me,
Let there be less of men and more of seals.—

ADAM

Oh Lucifer, let's go, I've had enough!

LUCIFER

But let us at least meet the fellow's wife.

ADAM

I've no desire to meet her. When man has touched
The depths, the very sight offends our eyes—
There's nothing but contempt left in our hearts.
But woman, that ideal, that poetry
Made tangible, when she descends so low,
Becomes deformed and monstrous to behold.
Let us go. I have no wish to see her.

In the meantime LUCIFER *has been dragging* ADAM *towards the hut and as he ends his speech, kicks in the door, where we find* EVE *as the Eskimo's wife.* ADAM *stands at the threshold, quite transfixed*

247

LUCIFER

Don't you recognize an old acquaintance?
Embrace her, it's the proper thing to do,
Her husband would take grave offence if you
Were not to show such courtesy to his wife.

ADAM

Embrace her, I, who held Aspasia
In my arms! This thing whose features hint
At some resemblance so contorted that
Somehow, in the very act of kissing
She's sure to be transformed into a beast.

ESKIMO
stepping into the hut

Guests, woman, be nice and friendly to them.

EVE *falls into* ADAM's *arms and pulls him into the hut*

EVE

You're welcome, stranger, come and rest.

ADAM
disentangling himself

Help me, Lucifer! Away from here,
Lead me from the future to the present,
Let me see no more of my harsh fate:
This useless struggle. Let me think it over
If I should I still take issue with God's will.—

LUCIFER

Wake then, Adam! Your dream is at an end.

SCENE 15

The scene changes back to that of Scene 3, a landscape with palm trees. ADAM *is once again a young man. He emerges somewhat sleepily from his cabin, and looks about him with amazement.* EVE *is dozing inside.* LUCIFER *stands centre stage. Brilliant sunshine.*

ADAM

Where have you gone, you dreadful images?
The world around me smiles and life goes on
As when I left it, but my heart is broken.

LUCIFER

Such dreadful vanity! Did you expect
The whole order of nature to collapse,
To find new comets blazing in the sky,
Or the earth to quake because one worm was lost?

ADAM

Did I dream it, or am I dreaming now,
And anyway, is life more than a dream
Which for a moment lights on inert matter,
Only to break up and perish with it?
Why grant us men an hour of consciousness
Only to show the horrors of unbeing?—

LUCIFER

Are you still grumbling?—It's pure cowardice
To accept defeat without a show of force
While a man still has the power to avoid it.
A strong man watches unperturbed while fate
Dictates its terms, letter by letter. He makes
No fuss, he sees the sentence written out,
And he can bear its weight upon his shoulders.

This is the fate that waits on history,
You're merely a tool: the process drives you onward.

ADAM

No, no—you're lying. We possess free will,
And I have more than earned its exercise.
I sacrificed all paradise for it,
And profited from what my dream revealed.
Many things have failed in disillusion,
It's up to me now to find better ways.

LUCIFER

Eternal hope, forgetfulness—if only
They were not in league with destiny,
So while the one is busy healing wounds
The other spreads a rug over the chasm
And exhorts you, saying—a hundred men have fallen,
But you, you'll be the one who leaps right over.
But you, as a man of science, will have seen
A host of curious things—recall that worm
Which lives only inside a cat or kestrel,
But nonetheless must spend the earliest phase
Of its life-cycle inside a common mouse.
No particular mouse is singled out
To feel the cat's claw, or the kestrel's talon,
One that is careful could avoid them both
And die at home, at a venerable age.
But there's an iron law which so requires,
That there be mice enough to go around
That even the defenceless worm survives
And prospers after many thousand years.
So individual men are not tied down,
But as a race they're forced to go in chains;
Floods of enthusiasm sweep them on
From one ambition to the next where some
Are fuel to the fire and others mockers.
And whoever keeps a catalogue of these

Must surely admire the sheer consistency
Of fate, which fixes marriages and deaths,
Governs the incidence of vice and virtue,
Of faiths and madness and of suicides.

ADAM

Enough, no more! O what a thought has struck me—
I can still defy you, God, yes, even You.
Though fate may keep repeating: Live so long!
I could laugh it out of court if I were dead.
For am I not alone in all the world?
There stands the cliff before me, there the drop:
One final leap, the last act of the play…
Then I may say the comedy is ended…

ADAM *moves towards the cliff.* EVE *emerges from the hut*

LUCIFER

The end, the end: what nonsense you do talk!
Each moment's a beginning and an end.
Was it for this you journeyed down the years?

EVE

Why steal from me so stealthily,
So cold embraced, so frigidly,
I see you're angry, deep distressed,
Oh Adam dear, you frighten me.

ADAM
continuing on his way

Why follow me, why guard my steps
So jealously? The lord of earth
Wants more than coddling. Women never
Understand a man. They bind him.

softening

Why could you not have slept a little longer:
It will be so much harder to perform
The sacrifice that time requires of me.

EVE

If you hear me it might be less hard.
For all is known that was in doubt
Of days to come. The secret's out.

ADAM

What is known, and how?

EVE

                          I know
How happy you will be, so hear,
I'll whisper low, oh come, come near—
I carry your baby, Adam dear.

ADAM
falling to his knees

My lord, you've conquered. I grovel in the dust;
I can't struggle without you or against you:
Raise me or strike me down. I bare my breast.

LUCIFER

You feeble worm! Have you forgot your greatness
For which you have me to thank?

ADAM

                                        Oh leave me!
The whole thing was a mirage: this is peace!

LUCIFER

And what have you to boast of, stupid woman?
Your son was conceived in sin, albeit in Eden,
And he'll bring sin and misery to the world.

EVE

If God so wills it, one will come
Conceived in misery and woe,
To wash the world and ring us round
With holy bonds of brotherhood.

LUCIFER

So you rebel against me, you mere slave?
Rise from the dust, you animal.

He aims a kick at ADAM. *The heavens open. The* LORD *appears on his throne, surrounded by* ANGELS

THE LORD

                    And you,
Spirit, down to the dust with you. There is
None great before me.

LUCIFER
stopping

        Curse the lot of you!

THE LORD

Adam, arise, do not be so downcast,
For see, once more I take you to my bosom.

LUCIFER
aside

A family reunion, I see.
All very nice for the emotions but
Unutterably boring for the mind.
I think I'll slink away.

He makes to go

THE LORD

      Wait, Lucifer!
I have a word to say to you as well.
And as for you, my son, tell me what ails you.

ADAM

My Lord, I have been racked by fearful visions,
And I cannot tell which of them is true.
Oh tell me truly, say what fate awaits me:
This little narrow life is all I have;
Is my spirit to be squeezed as in a press
Between my struggles, only for the wine
To be poured away at last into the soil,
Or have you other plans for this fine vintage?
Are we, our race, to steadily march onward,
Growing nobler as we approach Thy throne,
Or like oxen on a mill, exhaust ourselves,
Unable to break the leashes of our circuit?
Is there some recompense for noble spirits
Who shed their blood and face the ridicule
Of wretched crowds? O please, enlighten me,
And I will gladly carry any burden;
I cannot help but gain by knowledge since
Uncertainty is hell.—

257

The Lord

No, do not ask
To burrow deeper into the great secret
The hand of God, for the very best of motives,
Has hidden from your hungry eyes. For if
You knew the brevity of your existence
And were aware of heaven set beyond
Suffering would cease to be virtue.
If you could see the soil consume your spirit
What would spur you to shun the present good
For the sake of more inspiring ideals?
If now, with your future glimmering through the mist,
You bow beneath the weight of your ephemeral
Being, the sense of eternity will raise you.
And if the pride engendered by that snares you,
Your tiny span of life will set the bounds,
And safeguard virtue and nobility.—

Lucifer
cackling

Indeed, you have a fine career before you:
Nobility and virtue guide your steps.
Virtue, nobility—two words whose meaning
Is only realized when superstition,
Ignorance and prejudice provide
Their bodyguard.—Oh why did I embark
On mighty things with man who is mere mud
And sunlight rolled into a ball, dwarfish
In intellect, gigantic in his blindness.—

Adam

O Lucifer, refrain from mockery:
I saw the products of your intellect
And they were far too chilling for my heart.—
But oh, My Lord, who will be my guardian
To keep me on the straight and narrow path?
You left me free to taste the Fruit of Knowledge
But took away your guiding hand from me.

The Lord

Your arm is strong, your heart is elevated:
The field is vast and calls for endless labour,
And if you listen you will always hear
A voice to warn you or encourage you,
Pay heed only to that. And should it fade
Against the noise and bustle of your life,
This frailer woman's purer constitution,
Less muddied than yours with worldly interest,
Will hear it still and, passing through her heart,
The filtered voice will turn to poetry
Or music. With these instruments she'll stand
Beside you constantly, through fair or foul,
A smiling genius of consolation.—
And you too, Lucifer, you are a link
Within my universe—and so continue:
Your icy intellect and fond denial
Will be the leaven to foment rebellion
And to mislead—if momentarily—
The mind of man, which will return to me.
Your punishment though, which will be eternal,
Is ever to look on, and see your schemes
Of ruination turn into the seeds
Of all that is most beautiful and noble.

Choir of Angels

To make free choice of vice or virtue,
A proud ideal for man to bear
And still to know that God above us
Extends his shield with tender care.
Take courage then, expect derision,
Ignore the masses' howl of scorn,
'Tis not for their thanks that you labour,
When honour is of great deeds born,
All other action would be shameful;
It is the knowledge of his shame
That pins against the earth the wretched
But raises high the hero's name.

However your road may lead upward,
Do not be dazzled by the thought
That God is honoured by your efforts,
His Glory with your prowess bought,
Or that in some way He depended
On you to carry through His scheme:
Think rather that He does you honour
Allowing you to act for Him.—

EVE

I understand their song, praise God!

ADAM

I guess its meaning and will act upon it.
But for the end!—If I could but forget it!—

THE LORD

Man, I have spoken: strive on, trust, have faith!

———————

THE END

TRANSLATOR'S NOTE

One may approach a monument in many different ways. One may come bearing guidebooks, histories, gazetteers and encyclopaedias; one may approach from the most photogenic angle, on a spectacularly sunset evening; one may stop, make a brief tick on one's itinerary and move on. One may wish to avoid the vulgar crowds entirely and give the place a miss. Or one might walk round and around, venture in, take a deep breath and try to distinguish the various smells mingled in the walls. If enough time is spent there eventually the monument begins to feel like someone's home.

To extend my metaphor just a little, our last visitor will assume that local historians and archeologists will be far better informed than he on the subject of the monument, and he will not be tempted to take issue with them on documentary matters. A translator's preface will therefore spend little time on covering such ground. He does not presume to be a scholar. On the other hand, if he is a poet, he may try to describe the smell of the walls and list, in an adequately humble manner, discoveries which he will mistakenly believe to be his. His true discoveries will have been made less on the tour of the building than in the attempt to recreate it in a new setting. He is not Palladio but Lord Burlington, and if the result of all his labours is simply Timon's Villa he has failed.

Although Madách is in some senses an international figure he is hardly known in England—a fact that reflects probably more on England than on Madách. This being so one finds it hard to describe *The Tragedy* to an English reader. One might say, think of *Peer Gynt*, or think of *Faust*, or think of *Cain* but the reader will stand back somewhat abashed at the title. He may be accustomed to nineteenth-century ideology, even to nineteenth-century megalomania, but to discuss the ways of God to man after Milton seems a little ambitious to him. Being by temperament more sympathetic to mysticism than to ideology, he prefers, like Blake, his eternity in a grain of sand: a whole beach turns him into the Walrus or the Carpenter weeping to see such quantities of it wasted. His romanticism is a form of melancholy, a form of death-wish. He prefers it with sonorous music, not with arguments. It is a very long time since he last read Byron's poetry, apart from 'Beppo', or 'Don Juan'. He especially distrusts rhetoric and shrinks from displays of passion. If the play were called 'Adam's Dream' it might frighten him less.

So he will approach *The Tragedy of Man* with a certain mistrust. He will remember that Marlowe's *Dr Faustus* was the tale of a time traveller and intellectual voluptuary, who spoke in wonderfully vigorous verse. Adam is of course quite different. His passion derives not from Renaissance *hubris* but from nineteenth-century uncertainty. God is the *deus ex machina* who winds the world up then disappears, leaving the situation for man to sort out. Madách does not admit the possibility of communication between man and God. The friars and heretics of Constantinople are patently chasing shadows, and Adam as a crusader is more interested in chivalry than in Christ. God's reappearance at the end holds out less hope than the fleeting visit of an absentee landlord. Lucifer is not the lord of hell but the spirit of negation. It is the reproductive urge and the responsibility that entails which maintains the human couple. Their trials and tribulations spring out of the fact that they are misfits. Adam, while more voluble and more capable of taking decisions, carries the germ of Kafkaesque man, continually deflected from a nebulous errand. But one cannot stretch this parallel too far. Man's character is validated by the cliff on whose edge he stands in the last scene. That is no dream: the potential for annihilation is what gives the whole play its urgency. En route to the cliff the reader will encounter folly in many guises, a folly which is by its very nature vicious and terrifying.

Political, social and metaphysical uncertainty make for a dangerous world. The irony for Madách's protagonist is that he can be by no means certain that certainty would make it safer. Indeed all the hints we have are that it makes it worse. Those who are certain are shown time and again to be arrogant and blind. If this sounds familiar it is because Madách is standing on the threshold of the modern world himself, and in three scenes offers us prophetic visions of it. The phalanstery, outer space and the frozen wastes are instantly recognizable to a late twentieth-century imagination.

The English reader therefore may begin here. The play is a vision of how the world was, is, and will be. If he listens carefully it is his own voice he might hear.

*

The first important decision the translator of Madách's *Tragedy* has to make is whether he is going to try and match the surface of the nineteenth-century original. In order to do so he would have to concoct an English somewhere between Browning and Arnold, with welcome touches of Clough. However, if he does so, he must be aware that he will produce what is, in effect a pastiche, and furthermore, one that will be confined to the realms of chamber drama, in one small Central European cupboard of that tiny and obscure chamber that English readers assign to foreign works.

Translations of *The Tragedy* exist of course, the most readily available being Horne's of 1963. Horne was prepared to accept the limitations of archaic language and within its compass did well to maintain stylistic unity. This was precisely the problem with other translations. Those which opted for colloquial ease found it difficult to set a tone that remained both convincing, yet supple enough to accommodate Madách's rhetoric.

There is no reason why we should expect Madách to think and speak like a man of our century, but in taking the colloquial option myself I acted in the belief that the essence of the drama for an English reader must lie in the startling relevance and urgency of a number of Madách's arguments. Indeed, one might stretch a point and claim that the argument *is* the drama. If the machinery of the verse itself appears to creak on occasion we can accept it because the dramatic momentum is sufficiently powerful to carry us through. We feel throughout the play that the issues it raises were of vital importance to the author, rooted not only in the nation's immediate history but in his personal life. For this we can forgive him the liberties he takes with his historical locations: after all, his imagination is more at home with morality than with literal reconstruction. He *feels* the French Revolution and invents a Danton to articulate his feeling. He constructs a spectral London out of miscellaneous raw material and endows it with biergartens and wayside shrines. He is not interested in the place but in the social climate. It would be as pointless for a translator to attempt to verify the accuracy of Madách's Egypt or Greece or Phalanstery as to seek clocks in Shakespeare's Rome. The language does not change from place to place, the dialectic goes on, searching for a model society. Adam's dream is a dream, not a travelogue.

It is however a dream that in Hungarian has left behind a language endowed with proverbial force. I have never seen any point in producing a word-for-word translation if it does not provide an effect comparable to the original. Translation is metamorphosis: the translator must feel the quality of the original and find a formula that retains as much as possible of its contents while transforming its surface. He must present a living creature to his readers, not a corpse in national costume.

There is in this case no particular difficulty in recreating Madách's verse patterns, since in English the iambic pentameter has been the natural vehicle of narrative or philosophical poetry. From the baroque sonorities of Milton, through Wordsworth's 'Prelude', the broken columns of 'The Wasteland', down to our own day, it has been intermittently friend and foe to English poets. The very term 'blank verse' is enough to cast a deep depression over the British Isles. And yet no convincing substitute has been found: all other solutions carry the label of their makers' too conspicuously for general use. In any case a translation is not the occasion for tampering with tradition. But five thousand lines of blank verse would have been rather wearisome, and certainly sounded so to me after the first draft. For this reason I have introduced a little variation. While strictly maintaining the rule that rhyme should be rendered for rhyme—as much for the sake of proverbial force as for pedantic accuracy—I have given certain characters in certain situations a roughly alliterative four-stress line. The reader will notice that the scenes in and immediately out of Paradise are handled this way to create a contrast with the formal language of pentameters that follow. I have tried to let some of the stiffness and formality of this verse melt away as the drama approaches our own day. The language of Ancient Greece is intended to be stern, of the Eighteenth Century light and ornate, of revolutionary France ardent and rhetorical, of Victorian London racy and colloquial, and so on. The Eskimo, being a primitive creature, returns to a crude four-stress line, and Eve at the end speaks a more delicate version of the same, which infects Adam in his conversation with her. In all this I have kept an ear out for the needs of actors who are the logical performers of the drama. If the translation cannot always give them exciting lines to speak, it at least tries to avoid undue difficulties for them. The exigencies of performance should not dominate the translation but the possibility should be kept open.

In performance, of course, it is normal for the text to be cut, often quite drastically, but even an uncut *Tragedy* would survive as a piece of epic theatre. Epic theatre succeeds or fails by confidence and pace. Once the audience (or players) begin to doubt the necessity of this or that scene they find suspension of disbelief very difficult. It is less important for a modern audience to be overwhelmed by excursions into Wagnerian stage machinery than for them to be pitched from one state of tension into another.

Madách understands this instinctively and encapsulates it in the ambiguous figure of Lucifer, the most complex and most intelligent character in the play. Madách's 'spirit of negation' both leads and opposes. His 'cold and calculating intellect' is not above envying the childlike happiness of the couple in Paradise, or being tempted by the flirtatious Helena in Constantinople. His cynicism punctures moments of potential melodrama. We both welcome him and shrink from him. Without him Adam would be little more than a series of heroic costume changes. With him, Adam's attempts at nobility and virtue gain credence. Eve, while living up to Pope's categorization of women as "Matter too soft a lasting mark to bear", bears several temporary ones to powerful effect. The most sharply defined of these is Barbara Müller, whose resemblance to Madách's own wife, Erzsike, has often been noticed. Her other metamorphoses, as slave, matron, dreamer, nun, aristocrat, sanguinary, bourgeois, mother, primitive, and instinctive repository of poetry, provide the magnet for Adam's emotions. None of this will please the modern feminist.

There are only two other real characters in the drama. One is the amorphous and fickle masses, always an object of Madách's interest if not affection. Despicable when passive, dangerous when active, Adam's ideal society is not for them, but for the secret band of talents they may harbour. The sin of society is not that it politically suppresses many of its members, but that it prevents them from expressing their humanity. Once the masses have been reduced to a single Eskimo they are of no further interest.

The last character we may regard as a distinct entity is the leader of the masses. He may lead for the worse, as the agitator does in the Greek scene, or for the better, as St Peter does in the Roman one. The Byzantine patriarch, Emperor Rudolf, Robespierre, The Industrialist, and The Elder are all authority figures of one sort or another. The London scene sees a multiplication and fragmentation of these into salesmen, gypsies, landlords and students, and is for this reason the most spectacular and dynamic in the play.

There are a number of splendid set-piece speeches which the translator must regard as poetry and hope to render poetry in return. The Angelic Host in the first scene, Eve's speech about Adam in the second, Adam's description of the forces of nature sweeping by him in the third, the songs and St Peter's speech in Rome, Helena's account of being pursued by lusting crusaders in Constantinople, and many later speeches fall into this category. Lucifer's constantly do. These are a problem and a pleasure. Speeches which are merely part of the mechanism of the play are more awkward, since it is in these that the question of colloquial tone is most apparent. When faced with some of Adam's more sententious speeches it is difficult to avoid bathos (the air pocket of rhetoric). Adam is more likely than anyone else to show his nineteenth-century pedigree. But as I have already pointed out, to take up his invitation would result in pastiche. The antithesis to this is not necessarily a thorough-going contemporary diction, but one that allows opportunities for shifts of tone and level, within which the odd archaism might draw no more attention to itself than an antique statuette in an educated modern living-room. I trust that an air pocket may be less disturbing if approached in stages, gently. The translator should be a skilful pilot, able to alter height and even perform a few aerobatic feats without too much discomfort to the passengers.

GEORGE SZIRTES

ON MIHÁLY ZICHY

"Zichy, like Gustave Doré, is an extraordinary genius, a *portentum*, to use the Latin expression, a vulcano perpetually exploding with talent." With these words Théophile Gautier, the renowned writer and critic, recognized Zichy's exceptional capabilities as early as 1858, on his journey to Russia. Gautier considered Zichy as "one of the most astonishing artists we have encountered since 1830, that particular turning point in art."

Mihály Zichy was born in 1827 in the village of Zala in western Hungary. The artist came from an impoverished branch of the well-known family of counts. In Vienna he studied under Ferdinand Georg Waldmüller, one of the outstanding representatives of the Biedermeier style, who taught him to search for human depth as well as precise observation. Zichy's psychological acuity is already evident in his most significant painting of the Viennese period, the *Life Boat* of 1847, where he presents with dramatic force the tragedy of those adrift at sea. The picture shows the strong influence of French Romanticism, but Zichy was also affected by those Italian artists whose work he studied during his Italian tour of 1846. The autumn of the following year signalled a turning point in Zichy's life: he travelled to Saint Petersburg, where Waldmüller had recommended him for the position of art teacher to a relative of the Czar. He was later promoted to official court painter, and as such he made a number of drawings and water colours depicting various scenes from the life of the Czar and his court. Though owing more to labour than to inspiration, these works bring to life the festivities, hunts and orgies of the court, sometimes with a satirical sting. Court society, even the Czar himself, are often portrayed by Zichy as arrogant and vain. In his own interest and that of his children he had to undertake many petty commissions, like the fan painted for the Czarina or the deck of tarot cards designed for the Czar. Though even such menial works testify to Zichy's outstanding talent, he was continually aware of the curbs on his natural vocation. In addition he recognized that conditions in Russia were being propelled towards a crisis and he felt inclined to side with those who sought to instal democracy by way of a revolution. His position prevented him from raising his voice against the court and the Church. But his art, especially from the late sixties on, increasingly expressed his objection against national suppression and religious despotism, as is evident in such works as *Jewish Martyrs, Auto-Da-Fé* and *Messiah*. In the latter work Jesus appears as the Saviour driving out the fraudulent Christians along with the supercilious pope. The *Messiah* is presented as the liberator of a suppressed people. Not surprisingly the artist's standing at court gradually declined and it is more than likely that the court nobility spoke out against Zichy's revolutionary inclinations. It became increasingly clear that he had to leave Russia.

Betwen 1874 and 1879 Zichy was working in Paris, free at last from the burden of official commissions. The large canvases the artist painted at this time reflect the overwhelming impact the French capital had made on him. Here it became possible for him to deal with the problems of his age. He was inspired by the French, Russian, Polish, Czech and Belgian artists who became his friends. At the same time he presided over the Hungarian Society in Paris representing the interests of Hungarian workers and tradesmen there.

In these years Zichy completed his most significant painting, the *Weapons of the Demon (The Triumph of the Genius of Destruction)*, a monumental work intended for the Paris World Fair of 1878. With romantic fervour Zichy portrayed the inhumanity of those who opposed progress, and spoke out against the murders instigated by heads of Church and State who were possessed by the spirit of destruction. The artist was referring to specific events: the battle scene in the foreground is from the Russian-Turkish War, and in the background Napoleon III lies defeated on the ground in front of the Emperor, Wilhelm of Prussia. The focal point of this demonic vision is the figure of the pope, enthroned on a heap of the bones of the victims, incapable of arresting the senseless slaughter. Originally, Zichy had painted into the background the symbolic figure of the French Republic with a halo around her head, but later, giving in to his critics, he replaced her with a faintly outlined figure of Christ. The composition met with great indignation because of its provocative message and was rejected by the World Fair. When it was exhibited in Budapest the picture was fiercely denounced by the critics; the general public, however, was enthusiastic.

Zichy went on to paint more monumental works, such as the *Falling Stars* of 1879, symbolizing the tragedy of failure, and his striking *The Witching Hour* of 1880, which depicts skeletons rising from their graves at midnight. During this time Zichy was also illustrating literary works such as Mikhail Lermontov's *Demon* and Goethe's *Faust*. But Zichy always felt out of place, unable to cope with the disappointments he had had to endure. He slowly came to realize that in Russia he was more respected than in his own country, and—following shorter sojourns in Nizza, Zala, Vienna, Venice and Tiflis (Tbilisi)—he decided to return to Saint Petersburg in 1883. He was to remain there until his death in 1906.

Yet he always considered himself a Hungarian at heart, and he continued to make illustrations for works by Hungarian poets like Imre Madách's *The Tragedy of Man* and the ballads of János Arany. As he once said: "I consider it my patriotic duty to place my art in the service of our poetry and our poets." Illustration must be the condensed visual expression of intellectual content, and this precisely was Zichy's strength. His drawing is expressive and concise, his shading neatly balances light and dark, and his conceptions are dramatic. He possessed the intuitive gift of revealing new levels of meaning and mood inherent in his literary text, while at the same time introducing his own outlook on life. He always selected to illustrate the particular scenes that he could best identify with. This is especially evident in his illustrations for Madách's *The Tragedy of Man*.

Zichy began working on this subject in 1885. In this year, Czar Alexander III granted him a release from his duties for two months. In the months to come he completed fifteen illustrations. Later he made five more, so that the second, special edition of *The Tragedy* published in Hungary by the Athenaeum Press in 1888 already contained all twenty illustrations.

Zichy always made a number of sketches before embarking on his final version. His illustration for the Byzantine scene, for example, was preceded by six, and for the Prague scenes by eight preliminary sketches. He made no illustrations for the third scene, but for some others (Scenes Four, Seven, Twelve and Fifteen) he drew two and for Scene Six, the Roman Scene, he actually drew three.

In 1886, when the first fifteen illustrations were exhibited in the Budapest Art Gallery, they were received favourably right away. In the words of a contemporary critic: "Few poets have been better interpreted than Madách has by Zichy". In the 1892 performance of *The Tragedy of Man* in Vienna by the City Theatre of Hamburg the costume designs were based on Zichy's drawings. His originals were bought by the Hungarian National Museum through public funding in 1905, and are presently held in the Graphics Department of the Hungarian National Gallery.

The series comprises a number of charcoal drawings on 790 × 503 mm sheets. Each is a unique reinterpretation of Madách's concepts, each spurs the reader's imagination, each is an accompaniment to the literary work which it matches in artistic quality. *The Tragedy* was very close to Zichy's heart; he had always been inspired by the unusual, by phenomena which defy definition, by the world of dreams and tales, by ages far removed in time. At some points his message diverges from the author's, alleviating the poem's mood of pessimism, and occasionally, as in the Roman and Byzantine scenes, he adds details not included in the text. He was always careful to represent a given period with historical precision and his illustrations testify to a profound knowledge of history, ethnography and art. Dramatic unity and fine proportions give them an airy quality: the eye is drawn to the details, the striking effects of light and dark, and the ingenious draughtsmanship. There is no trace of theatricality or hackwork, as a later critic said about some of the pieces. On the contrary, the illustrations have a genuine pathos and demonstrate the artist's empathy with his material.

There have been passionate disputes concerning the status of Zichy's work in his own lifetime, and even today there is little agreement about the role and significance of his art. Gautier has already pointed out this artist's diversified character: "… a diverse nature; sometimes we think we know him […]; then suddenly we find ourselves facing a new work of his, and immediately everything we have just said is proven untenable." Criticism is primarily directed at his monumental oil paintings, their harsh shapes and bland colouring: he is accused of drawing even when he was painting. There may indeed be some validity in the charge that Zichy's idealism is often too abstract and his works too theatrical, but critics are unanimous in praise of his drawings, particularly his illustrations to works by Lermontov, Pushkin, Gogol, Goethe, Madách, Arany and others: these are considered outstanding and unique. He was clearly influenced by Hogarth, whom he greatly respected, and he possessed a fine collection of his engravings. His other influences included, for example, Goya, the French Romantics, the Belgian Wiertz. He was however able to assimilate them in a style and idiom that is recognizably his own, one which still awaits proper definition.

JÁNOS FALUS

CONTENTS